UNSCRIBBLING

the art of problem solving and fulfilling your desires

KRISTIN NEPERUD MERZ

TRANSFORM YOUR
SCRIBBLES ON A NAPKIN
INTO REALITY
BY EMPOWERING YOURSELF
WITH THE ART OF
PROBLEM SOLVING!

:)

Cover design by: Unscribbled, Inc.
http://www.unscribbled.com
(that's Unscribbled with an ed instead of an ing)
UnscribblED is the author's design business. UnscribblING is all about this problem solving book and the random musings of the author.

Published by: Unscribbled, Inc.
ISBN #: 978-0-9787629-0-2 or 0-9787629-0-8

Enjoy the fish!
(I realize that makes no sense to you now,
but when you get to the end it will.)
Notes from the Author

Notes from the Author

Becoming a problem solver is one of the most empowering things you can do for yourself. I applaud you for taking such a powerful step in your life, and thank you for giving me the opportunity to share in your journey. Unscribbling is a process, but please rest assured that no matter what your typical approach to problem solving has been in the past – whether you are the list-and-goals type or the spiritual type – the methodology and the layout of the book will be approachable for all types of personalities.

Although this book is about problem solving, I want to stress that I am in no way encouraging you to focus on your problems. Quite the contrary – by teaching you how to problem solve, I am encouraging you to focus on your intended results and create the life that you desire.

But before we go any further, I feel I must warn you that I once took a personality profile and part of it said: "She is usually polite but may sometimes be too frank, thereby leaving an aggressive impression." Being a "no-bull" type of person has definitely gotten me into trouble on more than one occasion. I try to be mindful of this in my personal interactions. However, since this book is not directed at any one person, I figure I can be as frank as I want to be here. So if you are up for a straightforward discussion on learning how to confront life's challenges and make your dreams and desires come true through the art of problem solving, please read on! If not… umm, maybe give this book to someone else. Either way, please consider yourself warned.

Also, I must clarify that although this book will delve into some armchair psychology at times, please note that I am not a trained psychologist; I am a trained designer who uses problem-solving skills every day. I have seen the principles outlined in this book work both personally and professionally, and I am hoping to pass them on to you here.

As you find your true desires and work to fulfill them, many emotions and feelings may come to the surface. I encourage you to use your emotions as a tool. If you have strong feelings of joy, anger, sadness, etc., explore that area of your life more – either on your own or with a trained professional. All of those emotions are good things. Your positive feelings are pointing you towards your happiness, and the negative ones are showing you areas in your life to work on. They are all helping you learn more about yourself, and the more you can learn about yourself the better.

Personally, I have found that the more I know about myself, the more I learn to accept myself. The more I accept myself, the more I am able to accept others as they are. As you learn to become more accepting individuals, others can learn and grow from your example. Our inner peace will start to spread.

My intentions with this book are that you will...

- Obtain peace of mind knowing that there are ALWAYS solutions to your problems and ways to attain your true desires.
- Gain confidence knowing that there is more than one solution to whatever situation you want to solve or change.
- Know a step by step approach that you can use so you don't have to rely on other people to solve your problems for you.
- Go out into the world with more confidence and with a feeling of worthiness, knowing that you are deserving and capable of making your desires and dreams a reality.
- Find the inner peace (and happiness) that comes with the confidence of a peaceful mind; and thereby create more inner peace and happiness in the world.

Best wishes on your journey,
Kristin

P.S. All names have been changed so that I don't break any implied confidentialities or hear any crap from anyone.

> *"Be the change you want to see in the world."*
> *- Gandhi*

Table of Contents

Introduction

Part 1 - What is unscribbling?
(The process)

Part 2 - Things to think about
while unscribbling

The Extras

Throughout the book you will find QR tags that link to various "Extras." To access the extras you can use either the QR tag or the link provided. Both will bring you to the extra located on the http://www.unscribbling.com website. (Tag reader can be downloaded from http://gettag.mobi)

Two types of extras are included:

1. Miscellaneous Extras

These include downloadable worksheets, links to more information, musings, and a few random fun things. These extras appear like this:

Extras
To see the entire list of extras, go to:
http://bit.ly/UExtras

2. The Spiritual Side Notes

Although I am a spiritual person, I am going to try to keep spirituality out of this book as much as possible. But, for the more spiritually minded among you, throughout the book you will find links to various "Spiritual Side Notes." The spiritual side notes will be distinguished from other "extras" with lines around the QR code and link, as shown below. All spiritual side notes can also be found at: http://bit.ly/SSN-list

SSN- Intro to the Spiritual Side Notes
To read your first spiritual side note, zap the tag to the left, or go to:
http://bit.ly/SSN-Intro

One more thing before you begin reading and unscribbling

We learn best by doing, not by just reading how to do something. Before you begin reading this book, please take a moment to write down three to five problems you would like to solve, or goals/desires that you would like to manifest in your life. You will use these "wants" to work through the unscribbling process as you go. Make them about you, not some beauty pageant answer like "world peace," or anything like that. Then, below your goal, list your "but," or what you feel is stopping you from obtaining your goal. As you progress you will unscribble things and get "butless," but for now let's add in your "buts" too.

Some examples we will be referring to throughout the book include:
- I want to own my own home, but I don't have enough money.
- I want to be in a relationship, but I don't have time to date.
- I want a job that pays well, but I would have to go back to school to get one.
- I want to lose weight, but I don't have time to work out.
- I want a baby, but I can't seem to get pregnant.
- I want to be a billionaire, but I only make $35,000 a year.

Other example goals to help inspire you include:
- I want to become a best-selling author.
- I want to take a trip to Italy.
- I want to get my pilot's license.
- I want to go back to school.
- I want to raise a well-adjusted child.
- I want to be famous.
- I want to leave my marriage.
- I want to plan the perfect wedding.
- I want to quit my job.
- I want to get a better paying job.
- I want to work at a place where the people are not all crazy.
- I want to lose weight.
- I want to own a Ferrari.
- I want to be a great husband/wife.
- I want my husband/wife to be happy.
- I want to move to a big city/the country.
- I want to make a difference in the world.
- I want to retire in five years.
- I want to get laid. (Yes, I did just list that. I don't judge your wants, and neither should you. Be honest with yourself as you write your list.)
- I want to learn to paint.
- I want to stop smoking.
- I want to become a _____.
- I want to have my own business.
- I want to learn how to cook.

If you are not sure what you want, that's okay! Keep reading, you might be able to find your wants in your frustrations (more on that later)....

Unscribbling Exercise 1

1. I want _____

   but _____

2. I want _____

   but _____

3. I want _____

   but _____

4. I want _____

   but _____

5. I want _____

   but _____

You can use the process in this book to tackle any problem you are facing, whether it be work or personal. You don't HAVE to come up with a list of things you would like to deal with – but it sure does help you learn and relate to the process. So I highly recommend that you "play along at home" with your personal list.

Introduction

In life, you can either become a victim of your circumstances and spend your life bitching, moaning and beating your head against roadblocks, or you can empower yourself. You can settle for where you are in life, or you can learn how to get past roadblocks and make your life all that you desire it to be.

This book will give you steps to help you find your true desires, explore ways to fulfill your desires, and create an actionable plan toward fulfilling your desires. It does this by demonstrating key problem solving strategies I have learned, and sharing observations that I have made over the years. The strategies and observations have helped me to "unscribble" problems in all areas of my life and develop what I call a "problem solving consciousness."

By developing a problem solving consciousness and knowing this process, I find that no matter what problems, roadblocks or detours show up in my life, they are in no way debilitating. They aren't, because I know that every situation in life that might stop me from progressing can be taken care of with some basic problem solving skills. Unfortunately, these are skills that are rarely taught in schools or at home. You may be taught how to solve "a" particular problem, but you probably have not been taught how to solve ANY problem that comes your way. The techniques in this book can be applied to any problem – big or small.

Although being able to solve your problems and fulfill your dreams is great, I have found that the biggest benefit of developing a problem solving consciousness is that you are free to thoroughly immerse yourself in the present moment, enjoy the flow of life, and find a peace of mind that comes with the confidence of a peaceful mind.

Now, don't get me wrong. By being peaceful and present in the moment, I am not suggesting that you spend the rest of your life meditating (unless you really desire to do that). Meditation is good –great, actually – but unless you are hooked up to an IV and a waste disposal system, there will be limits to how long you can do that. Even then, our bodies were meant to move. If you have the ability to move and do not take advantage of that, I feel you would be wasting a precious gift. The unscribbling process I am suggesting is a way to find some inner peace as you move about in the real world.

You will create a mental (and/or spiritual) state of being that allows you to stay calm and peaceful when faced with life's highs and lows. You can find that calm state of being in the real world by empowering yourself with the skills to solve whatever problems come your way.

For when you know how to solve problems, you are equipped with the ability to realize all of your true desires. Knowing that you are capable of making your desires come true makes the present so much more enjoyable. Instead of being frustrated that you cannot meet a certain goal or that you're not "there" yet, you can feel content knowing that if you truly desire it, there IS a way to achieve your desire. You can unscribble whatever you are facing! You just need the skills and the drive to do it. Then, it is just a matter of time before your desires are realized.

With unscribbling, life will become like reading good fiction – always wanting to know what happens at the end of the book, yet at the same time, when the story is really good, not wanting the book to end because you are enjoying the journey and the story so much. Similarly, you end up loving the present moment in your life, just as it is, as much as loving the moment when your desires are met.

The journey becomes all the more important if your desires change along the way. Which is often the case with new knowledge and clarity about the solutions you are pursuing.

"If you want to meet someone who can fix any situation you don't like, who can bring you happiness in spite of what other people say or believe, look in the mirror, and say this magic word: Hello!"
– Richard Bach

Takeaway: Unscribbling is a problem solving process that empowers you with the ability to tackle any problem that comes your way and to fulfill your dreams.

How is problem solving the key to fulfilling your dreams?

Problem solving is actually something that we all instinctively know how to do. We can easily apply problem solving in an emergency, but when it comes to our everyday lives, for some reason, we don't trust the process. As a result, we make life harder than it needs to be.

If you go back to your instinctive problem solving skills, you can find the framework to solve any issue that is facing you, even the problem of, "How do I fulfill my dreams?"

Think about it. When an emergency or crisis occurs, there is no time to form committees, gather our friends to discuss, or even worry and fret. In an emergency situation, you need to solve the problem and solve it as fast as you can. If you break down this emergency problem solving procedure, you get the model for how you can solve ANY problem that comes your way.

What happens when an emergency situation appears in our lives?

- First you BECOME AWARE of the problem: There is a strange man trying to get into the house uninvited.

- You declare or INTEND the state you desire to be in: To feel safe and not have a strange man come into the house.

- You BRAINSTORM solutions: I could pick up that baseball bat, or I could call the cops, or I could start screaming at him, or I could...

- You DECIDE, ACT and EXPLORE the best option(s) to pursue: I'll grab the bat and call the police. If that doesn't work, I'll start screaming and run out the back door.

- Then once the problem is solved, you THANK: the cops, your daughter for leaving her bat on the stairs, God, the Universe or whomever you believe in, and hopefully yourself too for getting through it.

During an emergency, as you ACT and you also stay OPEN. Open to alternative ways to get to your desired end state. Nothing stops you. If the phone lines don't work, you grab your cell phone, if the cell phone is dead, you open a window and start shouting. No matter what happens you keep pursuing your desired end state. You try option after option until something finally works and you have relief. And, if the police happen to be driving by before you call them, do you send them away so that you can follow the path you laid out for yourself? No! You get out of the way so this better solution can be allowed to happen. You are always staying open to better, faster, easier solutions.

This same procedure can be applied to ANY problem, and also toward improving, creating and living the life of your dreams.

1. BECOME AWARE
   You first notice a problem or area of your life you would like to improve.

2. INTEND

You see what you truly desire and set your intention towards fulfilling that desire.

3. BRAINSTORM

You brainstorm solutions to achieve your desired end state.

4. DECIDE

You choose a solution that you feel is the best.

5. ACT and EXPLORE

You take action and explore a path that will lead you to your desire. (You do all of this while staying open to other, possibly better, solutions.)

Then, when you solve the problem you...

6. THANK

You give gratitude for the results, and for any and all that helped you to get there. (Perhaps it's even your Oscar acceptance speech. Now who hasn't rehearsed that in their minds?)

This is the basic UNSCRIBBLING process. I call it unscribbling, because out of apparent chaos you can find order. Out of a scribble (desire) on a napkin, you can create reality. You can unscribble any problem you are facing, or achieve any desire you set your mind's eye on. You instinctively know how to do this. You just need to become consciously aware of the steps.

Sounds simple, doesn't it? Well, it can be when you learn and apply the process to your life. Those who apply the process will find they are living a life fulfilled. For whenever you are working towards your passion, your purpose, or your desires, you are living in a blissful state. It's not necessarily about achieving the end state (which you will); it's about enjoying the journey as you travel toward your desires.

"Everyone has to learn to think differently, bigger,
to be open to possibilities."
- Oprah Winfrey

Takeaway: Once you learn to consciously solve your problems, you will be unstoppable. You will be able to reach all of your true desires.

Step 1 Become aware

Before you transform, and before ANY unscribbling can occur, you must first become aware of the problem you are trying to solve. Seems obvious, but I have found that it really isn't. You need to look deeper than what is apparent to get at what you're REALLY trying to accomplish. You need to look beyond your wants, struggles, problems and goals to find your true desire. For at the heart of every problem there is an underlying desire.

What is the point of identifying your desires anyway?

Well, when you're living with fulfilled desires or confidently working towards the fulfillment of your desires – that's when you are HAPPY!!

They say you should, "follow your bliss!" Well, I say follow your desire and that is when you will find bliss. It's when you can't figure out what your desires are, or how to reach them, that you feel frustrated and unhappy.

In this section you will work to become aware of your true desires (or your bliss). Later, we will look at options to fulfill those desires. First, we need to find your true desire.

Searching for your desires

Sometimes we go through life unaware that there's anything we need to unscribble. People say "ignorance is bliss." I would beg to differ. If you don't deal with problems when they are small, they're bound to mushroom into big problems that you can't ignore, and those are harder to solve. If you deal with problems when they are small, you can get to your desired end state faster.

My guess is that on some level you are aware that you either have a problem you're not addressing, or you have a desire that you are not sure how to attain. Ignoring either is not going to make them go away, and it will keep you from your happiness.

So the first step in finding happiness through a problem solving consciousness is becoming aware that there is something in your life you want to change so that you can clearly define what you do desire your life to be like.

There are two places you can look to become aware of what you want to unscribble:

1. Your struggles/complaints
2. Your wants/goals (Which you previously listed in Exer. 1.)

In Step 1, we'll explore how to find the desires behind our wants and struggles – to become aware of the core of the problem you are trying to solve.

To me, finding the desire behind our wants and struggles is the biggest key to finding happiness through problem solving. For that reason, this section will be the longest, and the most emotional for some readers. The rest is easy problem solving skills. This first step of becoming aware of your actual desire – this is the tricky part! Don't worry. We will unscribble this together.

Let's start to look for your desires by examining how…

Struggles are here to help

Most people do not welcome struggles or problems in their lives. But problems, struggles and new desires nagging at you are natural to your personal development and evolution. Those frustrating feelings are actually here to help you; they are clues telling you to make adjustments in what you're doing. When you look at struggles this way, your frustrations stop feeling like something that is stopping you, and merely become emotional clues leading you to make adjustments in your life.

Just as your body sends pain and discomfort signals to compel an adjustment in your physical condition, your emotions are signals that tell you to make adjustments in your life. My bladder sends me discomfort and I know its time to "make an adjustment" and use the restroom. My back sends me pain and I know I need to stretch or maybe even go to the chiropractor to get a major readjustment. We listen to our physical bodies, but we need to remember to listen to our emotional bodies too.

When you start to feel your gut turn and you hear those nagging voices in your head saying: "I'm frustrated! This does not feel right! I'm not happy!" these feelings are signals from your internal guidance system. These negative feelings are telling you to make an adjustment in your life. Once the adjustment is made and you've adjusted your course, you will feel better.

When you choose to see your struggles as a signal, frustrations and problems become opportunities in disguise; clues to make adjustments and take your life in a new direction. That can be exciting!

When you feel yourself become frustrated, ask yourself, "What is it I DO want?" When you identify the "want," you bring yourself one step closer to identifying your true desires.

"Your life does not get better by chance, it gets better by change."
–Jim Rohn

Takeaway: Struggles, or negative feelings, are clues from your internal emotional guidance system encouraging you to make an adjustment.

SSN– Your Emotions Are Communication
http://bit.ly/SSN-Emotions

SSN– Frustrations and struggles are here to help.
http://bit.ly/SSN-StrugglesHelp

Let's look at your frustrations and struggle to try to get closer to some of your desires…

Unscribbling Exercise 2:

List areas of your life where you are struggling or feel frustrated. Then ask yourself, "What do I WANT that area of my life to look like?"

1. I am frustrated with _____

_____

I want _____

2. I am frustrated with _____

_____

I want _____

3. I am frustrated with _____

_____

I want _____

4. I am frustrated with _____

_____

I want _____

5. I am frustrated with _____

_____

I want _____

From your wants, you will figure out your true desires...

Setting goals versus pursuing your desires

I need to clarify something here. This is NOT a goal setting book. However, investigating your goals and wants can help you unlock the secret of what your true desires are by looking at their essence. So let's explore the idea of wants and goals versus your desires.

So, what is the difference between goals (or wants) and desires? Well, goals & wants tend to be specific solutions or benchmarks – rigid, unchanging and tangible. Something like:

- I want to be promoted to manager by the time I am 35.
- I want to be married by the time I am 28.
- I want to own my own home.
- I want kids of my own.
- I want to retire by the time I am 62.
- I want to be a billionaire.

But.... What happens if you are unable accomplish them in the timeline that you thought you should, or if they don't work out at all?

Life is fluid, unpredictable and constantly changing. The rigidity of goals can send you into a tailspin if, say, your fiancé dumps you at age 27, or a parent becomes ill and you need to financially support them, or you are unable to conceive a child, or the economy crashes and your retirement investments take a plunge.

Technically, you might still be able to meet your goals, but is that going to be what is best for you? You might be able to rustle up someone and still get married by the time you're 28, but is he or she going to be the right person for you? You might still be able to retire, but will it be the kind of retirement you enjoy?

If life throws you a curve ball (as it often does), what happens to your goals? Do you throw them out the window? Push back the timeline? Get angry with God, because God has not answered your prayers? Play the victim? Dive into that pity party? What happens when you can't solve the problems you are facing or meet your goals?

You want to be married, you want to make more money, you want life to be easier, etc. When you have the want, and no way to meet it, it's natural to feel frustrated. Once we feel that frustration, we tend shut down. We end up doing nothing, or we bitch and moan to our friends about how rough we have it. We focus on our lack and on the problem, not on the solution and the good that is present; thereby getting us nowhere.

All in all, goals are not bad. It's when we get stuck on them and lose sight of the desire behind them when goals start to do us a disservice. The good news is that behind each of your goals and wants is a hidden desire – the underlying wish or longing that brought it into being.

Instead of rigid goals, look at the desires behind the goals/wants. Like:

- I desire to have a career that uses my gifts and compensates me fairly.
- I desire a loving companion in my life.
- I desire to be financially prepared for my future.
- I desire to love and be caring towards another.

It is not just a matter of changing the word "want" to "desire." It's about finding the true desire behind the want.

Think about your goals/wants and desires as if you WANT to book a flight from New York to San Francisco, but the airlines are grounded due to bad weather. So you end up taking a train. Along the way, the train breaks down in Chicago. So you end up jumping on a bus. But there is a whole section of I–80 that is torn up, and you end up taking I–70 instead. However, the bus driver will not go past Las Vegas (something about bad mojo and he doesn't want to risk his luck on the tables). Since they can't get another driver in for two days, you end up renting a car to drive the rest of the way. You WANTED to take a flight to San Francisco, but when that did not work out, you did not lose sight of your true desire – to get to San Francisco. You had to use alternate routes than you had planned, and you might have gotten there on a different timeline, but ultimately you still got there.

In this scenario, your goal/want was to take a FLIGHT to San Francisco. The true desire behind it would be to get to San Francisco.

Once you know your true desire, it opens up a world of possibilities. If it is your true desire, there will be no roadblocks to accomplishing it; perhaps a few detours and paths that seem surprising, but never a complete dead end. You won't let there be a dead end because you know that there is always more than one way to fulfill your desires!

> *"When a child screams, 'I want my doll!' is it the doll, or love and comfort they are looking for?"*
> *— Anonymous*

Takeaways: Wants/goals are just some solutions that can help you meet your true desires.

Goals are rigid benchmarks, desires are helping to guide you to your happiness.

SSN– Focus on Your Desire, NOT Your Problem
http://bit.ly/SSN-LOA

So don't strive for achievements?

Definitely strive! Just know what you are REALLY striving for and stay flexible on how you get there. I am not saying to not get married, work towards a promotion or have kids. Just look at what you REALLY want and don't keep yourself locked on only one way to accomplish it. Marriage, kids and new jobs are all great solutions to your desires, but there are many other solutions that might work too. Opening yourself to those possibilities will make life a heck of a lot less stressful and more interesting.

For instance, I never set a goal to "get married." I did, however, desire a mutually supportive loving relationship. If that someone happened to be someone I enjoyed making out with – all the better! Because of this, I have always had supportive loving companions in my life; sometimes just as friends, sometimes I could smooch on them too.

Then I found this guy who was a supportive loving companion, fun to be around, pretty darn cute and a good kisser to boot! After awhile, it became clear that we desired to make this a permanent relationship. ONE way to do this was to get married. There are other ways, too. But we decided that marriage was the way that best fit us.

When we decided to get married, we had to start planning the wedding. We wanted the wedding to be on the beach. That did not work out. I wanted my friend to be my "best woman." She declined, as she said she would be too pregnant to stand up during the ceremony. I wanted a solid wedding ring about .5 inches wide. Turns out my hands are too clammy to wear a ring like that. Tried it. On me, a wide ring was like wearing a wet band–aid all the time – yuck! Once upon a time I wanted a different man up there with me. Thank God that didn't work out. (No offense to the guy(s).)

What I got instead was a wedding in a gorgeous mountain area with rolling hills; my sister as my "best woman" (who was amazing and I was able to bond with on an even deeper level than before); the help and presence of my pregnant friend anyway; a super cool artsy ring; and a guy so great for me that I count my blessings for him every day.

For every part of our wedding, nothing was what we originally thought we "wanted." Instead, it turned out that everything was beyond perfect, because our true desires had been met.

It was perfect because we stayed open to our true desires.

My true desire initially being:
- To find a great companion for myself.

Then, once we decided to get married, our desires were:
- To find a way to do that in the presence of the people we love.
- To celebrate our marriage in a way that fit our personalities.
- To have a great time.

All of our true desires had been met! We had a fabulous time, and I could not stop smiling the whole day!

If I had held on to what I thought I "wanted," and tried to problem solve and make them happen, I would have been miserable and disappointed. (Know any Bridezillas?) By not diving into a pity party every time something happened differently then what I had wanted, staying open to other solutions, keeping my/our desires in mind, and trusting that things would work out, more perfect answers arrived. By keeping my true desires in mind, everything turned out to be fabulous.

So, as life gives you lemons when you thought you wanted oranges – go with it. It might be leading you to something wonderful! Like lemonade, or lemon sherbet, or limoncello, or lemon meringue pie, or a new lemonade selling business, or... just think of the possibilities! Or go to www.epicurious.com. There you will find over 4,000 recipes that use lemons. I am sure you can find something good to do with them.

Instead of lamenting those oranges you wanted but did not get, follow your true desires and stay open to the new blessings and opportunities. Dream of the all the possibilities, but wish for "that – or something BETTER!" You will be astonished at what comes into your life.

"You can't always get what you want... but you get what you need..."
–Rolling Stones

Takeaways: As you work toward your desires in life, stay open to other solutions that might fulfill them.

Instead of resisting the situation that is, embrace it and move toward your true desire from whatever point you are at.

OR...

As Mark Twain wrote, "There is more then one way to skin a cat." Just make sure "skinning a cat" is what you really desire to do. (Who would want to skin a cat?)

When life gives you lemons, don't cry about it; lemons might be leading you to something more wonderful then you ever imagined!

EXTRA: Why do I embrace desires?
http://bit.ly/Extra-Desires

EXTRA: Why not just set a goal and go for it?
http://bit.ly/Extras-NotGoals

Finding your desires through "problem seeking"

Now that you have identified some of your wants, you can become aware of your true desires through a process called "problem seeking." Problem seeking is all about getting to the heart of a problem BEFORE you even think about trying to solve the problem. So let's "problem seek" your way to the heart of your wants and identify your true desires.

What is "problem seeking"?

I was first introduced to this concept in college. Part of the recommended reading for the Environmental Design class at University of Wisconsin–Green Bay was the book Problem Seeking by William M. Peña and Steven A. Parshall from the architectural firm HOK (Hellmuth, Obato and Kassabaum). The book's intention was to aid architects in communicating with their clients in the pre–design phase.

The book outlines a method of discovering the true goals and desires for the buildings they were designing before they started designing what it would look like. Peña and Parshall's method first examined a "problem" and then identified the root of what they were really trying to accomplish with the building. Only after the core problems and desires were discovered do they start looking for solutions.

I admit, grasping this concept of looking behind the problem was difficult, but when I saw how problem seeking works, my life was changed. This concept has since shaped the way I do just about everything – especially the way I conduct my design business. In my design business, I am constantly searching for my client's true objectives, then brainstorming ways to solve what they are really trying to accomplish with their website, brochure, logo, etc.

For instance, a client once requested that I create a giant hand pointing to a feature on their website. Knowing that they had an upscale clientèle, my design taste buds puckered. After the initial disgust and shock wore off, we talked and concluded that what he really wanted was to draw attention to the offer. Whew! There were a lot of ways we could do that: highlight it, use a contrasting color, enlarge the type font, move it to a more prominent location, etc. Anything would have been better than that giant hand. By asking "why" he wanted that giant hand, we found the desire or "heart of the problem," then found a better solution.

(P.S. The questions: "Why" and "Why not?" are some of the most powerful questions you can ask. See the link at the end of this chapter for more on this.)

In college, we applied the techniques from the Problem Seeking book when our class was designing initial concepts for an art center for the Sovereign Oneida Nation of Wisconsin. One of the things we thought we wanted in the building was an art gallery. Makes sense, since it was an art center. We could have just added in a standard gallery to some corner of the building, perhaps off the lobby, called it done and gone for a beer at the campus pub. But problem seeking forced us to think about the true purpose of a gallery a little bit more. We had to take a step back, look at the true objectives of an art gallery, and then we were able to go forward with multiple solutions.

To go one step back, we asked ourselves: "Why do we need an art gallery? What exactly is the purpose of an art gallery? What do we desire to accomplish with this?" The answer was, "to have a way to safely display art." So we did not necessarily need an "art gallery," but a way to safely display art. After we got to the true heart of what we wanted, or our true desire, then we could start to brainstorm possible solutions. An art gallery was only one solution to the problem.

The answer I liked best was to have art on display in all of the hallways throughout the new art center – perhaps behind protective glass if needed. By having the art throughout the facility, we were mirroring how the Oneida incorporated art in all aspects of their lives. The whole building would then become a gallery with art integrated everywhere. We might not have gotten to that scenario unless we took a step back and looked at the true problem or desire before solving for it.

Once you open yourself up to the notion of getting to the heart of an issue, that original want or "goal" usually becomes just one solution of many. As with my client, the hand pointing to the feature was one solution of many possibilities. As with the art center, a gallery was one solution for how to display art.

So, before you do any problem solving, or pursuing your desires, begin by becoming aware of the heart of the problem or desire. Seek the true problem by looking beyond the goal and find the true desire of what you want.

"Problem solving is a valid approach to design if indeed the design solution responds to the client's design problem. Only after a thorough search for pertinent information can the client's design problem be defined or stated. 'Seek and you shall define!' "
–From Problem Seeking by William M. Peña and Steven A. Parshall

As you look for your desires, your want may change from:
I want to get a job.
to
I desire to create a stream of income for myself.
I desire to put my talents to use.
I desire to use part of my day interacting with others.

Takeaway: Finding the heart of your problem or desire opens up a world of possibilities to accomplish it.

EXTRA: The power of "Why?" and "Why not?"
http://bit.ly/Extra-Why

SSN– Wants Keep You Attached
http://bit.ly/SSN-Attached

"Rules" to keep in mind about identifying your desires

As you look for the desires behind your wants and problems, there are a few things you should keep in mind. Including:

Desire Rule #1 – Make your desires about YOU and how your desires affect YOUR life

Something to keep in mind as you look for your desires is that problem solving and seeking your desires is not about changing other people. You can lead by example, but you can only change yourself.

You might tell whomever is bothering you that you don't appreciate a behavior of theirs and politely ask them to do something else, but you cannot force them to stop their behavior. You can, however:

- Change how you relate and react to their behavior.
- Change the amount of contact you have with them.
- Change your attitude about the situation. (See Part 2, Chapter 7 – "Change Your Attitude.")

Unless you are the parent and the person in question is a minor, it is not your job to change or even guide another unless they have requested it. (Unsolicited guidance from parents is even debatable at times. Ask yourself if you are guiding your child to be the best person they can be, or to merely act in a manner that pleases you.)

If you have not been asked to guide another, I would even go one step further and say it also means not to even "pray that they become a better person." For how do you know that they are wrong and you are right? After all, do you pray for the homosexual, or for the homophobic? It will all depend on your perspective.

> *"You may give them your love but not your thoughts,*
> *For they have their own thoughts...*
> *You may strive to be like them,*
> *but seek not to make them like you."*
> *– The Prophet, by Kahlil Gibran*

Keeping this in mind, your want may change from:
I want to make my child a better person.
to
I desire my child to cultivate their uniqueness.

Takeaway: Work to change ONLY yourself.

EXTRA: The "Golden Rule" is Messed Up
http://bit.ly/Extra-GoldenRule

SSN– Work to Change ONLY Yourself
http://bit.ly/SSN-ONLYyou

What about when someone is harming someone else? Shouldn't I do something about that?

If the person being harmed or doing the harming is asking for help, or is a minor or otherwise unable to act for themselves, of course, help them out in whatever way you can (keep your health and safety in mind). But if the person is not asking for help, they are probably not emotionally ready to change the situation (See the

Part 2, Chapter 3 – "Playing it 'safe' and staying in your problem"). When one has suffered enough, one will work to change their situation. They may need help once they make up their mind, but until they identify THEIR desire to create a different situation, the change won't stick.

Domestic violence is a sad, but glaringly true example of this. I was once in a relationship with an emotionally controlling man. Emotionally controlling people are so subtle and stealthy about it you can be up to your eyeballs in love with a complete ass before you know it. They work very insidiously to make you think that you need to change to make them happy.

I kept trying to change myself to make my boyfriend happy (to change him). I did everything to reassure him that I loved him and there was no need to be insecure. It was never enough. There finally came a moment when I had enough. Once I had enough of dealing with his insecurities and changing myself to try to change and reassure him, I stopped. I then started focusing on being whole, happy, healthy and vivacious again. I knew I loved him. I had to stop trying to change his mind that it was true. I had to stop trying to change his feelings. I started to make my desires about me and worked to make myself the best person I could be. My letting my light shine and letting others see it too, was not something he could handle, and he left my life.

Along the way, no matter how many people tried to help, encourage me to leave, or make the situation better, THEY could not change ME. It was not until I desired the change strongly enough and gave myself permission to "write him off" if necessary that change was possible.

I'm not saying not to give advice to a friend. For you never know what advice is going to help. So give advice when asked. But, let that friend live the way they choose until they clearly desire something different. DON'T try to change another. They will change if and when they want to.

For me, the light bulb switched on when I heard that one of my boyfriend's friends said, "Why is she putting up with it?" Wow! If his friend could say that, then maybe this wasn't "normal" and I should not try to hold on to something that felt so wrong.

"Maybe they should have suffered a little MORE. Maybe they ought to touch rock bottom and say, 'I am sick of it all.' It's only when you're sick of your sickness that you'll get out of it. Most people go to a psychiatrist or psychologist to get relief. I repeat; to get relief. Not to get out of it."
— Awareness, by Anthony de Millo

By NOT trying to change another, your desire:
I want to make my husband happy.
may be changed to:
I desire to be happy.
I desire to be healthy.
I desire to express myself as I deem appropriate.
I desire to love my partner.
I desire a mutually supportive relationship with my spouse.
I desire to be the best person I can be.

Takeaway: A person's desire to change must come from him/ herself, not from you.

EXTRA: Writing some people off
http://bit.ly/Extra-WriteOff

SSN– Another's desire to change, must come from them, but…
http://bit.ly/SSN-Anothers

Side Note: Interventions, good or bad?

This is an issue that rips at my heartstrings. My close friend Sophia's dad is an alcoholic. He is slowly killing himself with alcohol. Most nights he drinks to the point where he passes out at the kitchen table and spends the night there... unless he falls on the floor and sleeps it off there instead. My logical mind says, "until he wants help, there is nothing they can do." My heart says, "they can commit him to a treatment program against his will with only three signatures and proof he is a danger to himself or others. It's the best thing for him."

Interventions are like giving advice: I encourage you to do it even if the person might not listen. Sometimes you have to do it for your own peace of mind. You have to know that you said your peace. You tried.

You could say, "You are killing yourself. I want you to be healthy and happy. If you want to get sober, you are going to need help. One way you can do that is by checking yourself in for treatment. We are here for you. We love you. We all want to see you get healthy and happy and living life to the fullest." Know that they might not do anything with your advice. No matter how heartfelt a speech you give them, they may choose their addiction over recovery. That is their choice.

But to commit someone against their will, or not, is the real question. I think this is something that can only be answered on a case-by-case basis and with lots of input and perspectives. This is a bigger issue than one person insisting that another change.

Typically, it takes three people to commit someone. I respect and appreciate the fact that it takes three signatures to even start the process of committing someone. It has to be more than just one or two people who feel a need to intervene in someone's life in such a dramatic way. These check and balance systems for interventions are beyond value.

Therein lies the key as to when to take drastic actions: Do at least three people think he is a potential harm to himself or others? Are his doctors in agreement? Does the judge think there is enough evidence that this is necessary? It takes ALL of those people to decide if it is right to try to make a change in someone else's life that they are not asking for. That is the process that should be used before trying to intervene in someone else's life.

Takeaway: Intervention in another's life is a drastic step and should not be the sole decision of one individual. If someone is a potential harm to themselves or others, follow the system of checks and balances to make sure interfering is the correct thing to do.

Desire Rule #2 – Make sure you are pursuing YOUR desire, not someone else's

In your search for your desires, it is vitally important to make sure that your desires are YOUR desires and not those of someone else, or of society. When you start to pursue desires that are not your own, things will go amuck.

One of my first employers out of college, Karen Raymore, used to humorously say, "You have to be who you is." When you are not being your true self, you're not going to be content or enjoy life. Plus it takes a TON more energy to be fake then genuine, so you might as well just be yourself.

> "...Professor Steve Cole of the University of California in Los Angeles proved our bodies benefit when we accept ourselves. He studied 200 homo-

sexual men over five years. He found the incidence of cancer and other disease was three times higher among those who hid their sexuality. Other studies have found that to function at our best, with healthy immune systems, we need to feel authentic, true to ourselves – even if we risk the disapproval of our peers."

– David Servan–Schreiber
Ode Magazine, Dec 2008

If you are gay and you believe that your desire is to meet someone of the opposite sex and settle down... honey, that is NOT going to work for you! It must, and can ONLY be your own true desire that you follow. Otherwise, even if a "desire" is met, you won't be happy. There is no point in that! Not being yourself is like eating foods you hate. You may be able to choke them down, but is that really how you want to live? Do you want to "choke down" your life, or savor it?

"A musician must make music, an artist must paint, a poet must
write, if they are to be ultimately at peace with themselves.
What a man can be, he must be."
–Abraham Maslow

Keeping this in mind, your desire may change from:
I desire to get married and have children.
to
I desire to be in a loving romantic relationship.
I desire to "fit in" with my peers.
I desire to create a life that I enjoy living .

Takeaway: Be YOURSELF and follow YOUR desires.

Who cares what your mother's friends think?

SSN – You can only be you
http://bit.ly/SSN-BeYou

Side Note: So, who are you?
Why are you here?
What is the meaning of your life anyway?

Ah, the eternal debate! We will never have an irrefutable answer, so let's stop trying to get everyone to agree, and agree to disagree. Instead of arguing, let's look to that sage wisdom, "Opinions are like assholes, everyone has one." In that statement we find a pearl of wisdom: your life's meaning, your life's purpose, who you are and what you stand for, is, and can be, whatever you decide it to be.

Perhaps you embrace the views of your religion, perhaps you have the view that there is no meaning to life at all, or perhaps you have no idea what you think and your first desire is to know the meaning for your life. Whatever works for you is the right answer. Like your desires, the meaning of your life may change as you and your life situations change. The purpose you attach to life at any given moment, and the way you define yourself can help guide you to discovering your true desires and how to fulfill them. I encourage you to explore what you feel is your purpose in life and who you uniquely are, as it will serve as an excellent guidance system as you face new challenges and desires in life.

I have a theory that perhaps instead of one pat reason for our existence, we are actually here to:
- fulfill a role within the greater whole
- grow as an individual through our experiences
- enjoy life

Keeping in mind that we may be here to fulfill a role within the greater whole, we are created with specific natural abilities. Whether these abilities are "God given," genetic, environmental or a product of chance, it does not matter. You got what you got, now deal with it. Better yet, EMBRACE IT!

By embracing, developing and using our natural abilities, our "purpose in life" will be fulfilled. Hiding your gifts or forcing yourself to follow a path society deems more acceptable goes against the nature of the universe and your true desires.

During one of the slow periods of my business, someone tried to encourage me to become a dental hygienist. Being concerned for my well being, she cited how hygienists, "make a lot of money and it's steady work." The "a lot of money and steady work" sounded appealing, but.... does she know me? My natural abilities are creativity and problem solving. How would that fit with being a dental hygienist? Perhaps I could reinvent a way to clean teeth. I might enjoy that, but – love the hygienists in the world – I could not in a million years do what they do and be happy. However, I am grateful for hygienists who express their natural abilities of being precise, thorough, caring and personable.

I say, stay within your budget or get a part time job if you have to. Be responsible, but NEVER give up on your natural gifts.

You could argue that you can develop any ability, but let me ask you, would you enjoy that? Or do you enjoy life when you feel "in the zone" while doing things? When you feel like you are truly being yourself, and when you are humming along at things you enjoy?

I feel so fabulous when I am using my natural gifts –
when I am creating, designing, problem solving, listening to
others and finding patterns and possibilities. Some may feel
that I should try to be a more well-rounded person and try
to develop those skills that I am not as good at. But, why?
How does my trying to hit a home run make the world, or
my life, better? (Except for the comic relief that might result
by watching me try.)

I highly recommend that you stay true to your natural
gifts in your business responsibilities as well. My friend, Todd
Smart, owner of BeTuitive, advised making the following
lists before you hire someone:

1. All the things you suck at
2. All the things that you are neither here nor there at
3. All the things that you are good at
4. All the things you are exceptional at

The first person you hire is the one who does all the
things you suck at, the next hire would do all the things you
are indifferent to, then the things you are good at. You are
left with always doing the things you are exceptional at. Can
you imagine how happy and productive you would be?

Don't feel bad about handing off the work that you don't
like. Your list of tasks that you enjoy is completely different
than other people's lists. The person you hired to do the
things that you suck at, those are the things they are exceptional at (hopefully anyway) and they are happy doing those
tasks.

There is no way one person is capable of developing and
maintaining every talent. Thus, we have evolved as an interdependent species. You may know a lot about a lot of stuff,
but there is no way you can do everything on your own.
Follow YOUR talents and desires, not anyone else's. They
are uniquely yours – so to recap Karen Raymore's phrase
once again, "be who you is!"

"For the meaning of life differs from man to man, from day to day and from hour to hour. What matters, therefore, is not the meaning of life in general but rather specific meaning of a person's life at a given moment."
— *Viktor E Frankl, Man's Search for Meaning*

Keeping this in mind, your desire may change from:
I desire to get a steady job that pays well.
to
I desire to work in a way that is abundantly fulfilling.
I desire to earn a living (perhaps you do the things you love at another time).
I desire to do work that is in keeping with my ethics and beliefs.

Takeaway: Be who you is!

SSN– Your Purpose in Life
http://bit.ly/SSN-LifePurpose

Desire Rule #3 – Don't judge your desires

Identifying your desires can be difficult if you don't want, or are afraid, to admit to yourself what they are. PLEASE do not judge yourself or your desires during this process, just look at your answers and stay open to what your true desires might be.

Judgment of your desires is really either:
1. Deeming your desires unworthy of you, or
2. Deciding you are unworthy of your desires.

NEITHER of those thoughts of unworthiness will get you anywhere.

When I say "unworthiness," I mean thoughts like:
- I can't do that. I'm not smart enough or strong enough.
- People who grew up where I did don't do that sort of thing.
- You have to go to graduate school to get a job like that.
- I don't deserve this.

Every judgment of unworthiness stops you from pursuing the things that might make you happiest. When you find yourself judging your desires or thoughts you are essentially letting all of the air out of your tires before you set out on a trip. That's not going to get you very far!

My friend Charles and I were talking about what his ideal job would be if he could do anything. With a contained smile, he said, "I'd love to be a copywriter for a sitcom or late-night TV show." As soon as he said it, I could see it – it made so much sense! He has a wicked sense of humor and a flare for comedic observation.

So my question was, "Why aren't you pursuing that? It's perfect for you!"

He put on his aw–shucks face, shook his head, and said, "Ahh... because that's not a responsible path to pursue. Besides, you have to be in your young twenties to pursue that. You have to start as an intern and work your way in. It's the only way."

I was tempted to throw my beer in his face and say, "What the hell are you thinking!" I didn't, but I wanted to. He had just squashed his dreams with two big judgments of unworthiness.

1. He judged his desire as "not responsible."
   (The desire was not worthy of him. NOT TRUE!)
2. He judged himself as too old.
   (He was not worthy of the desire. Again, NOT TRUE!)

Let's look at #1: "Not a responsible path." Huh? How is pursuing your dreams not being responsible? More likely he figured he'd be living in a tight budget during his internship, and that would be difficult. OR, probably more likely, he figured women might not find a man on a budget as attractive as a guy with a "responsible" job that pays well. NEWS FLASH: Women love men who pursue anything with passion! And if the woman is just looking for a meal ticket, do you want to be with her anyway?

#2: "Too old." Puleeze! He was only 31! If you want something badly enough, you are never too young or too old.

True desires, like people, are not "good" or "bad" they just are. If you desire it, you are worthy of your desire and your desire is worthy of you.

> *"I don't judge others. I say if you feel good with what you're doing, let your freak flag fly."*
> *– Sarah Jessica Parker*

Your inner "freak" is what makes you – you! LOVE it! Embrace it!

As you look for your desires, your want may change from:
I want to be a writer on a sitcom.
to
I desire to creatively express my humor.
I desire to earn an income through my gift of writing.
I desire to make people laugh.

As you look for your desires, your want may change from:
I want to be responsible.
to
I desire to be attractive to to the opposite sex.
I desire to be financially comfortable.
I desire to please my parents. (Delve deeper into this one if it's resonating with you. Pleasing others is like changing others.)

Takeaway: If you desire it, you are worthy of your desire and your desire is worthy of you. Don't let judgment stop you before you even get started.

SSN– Where did your desire come from?
http://bit.ly/SSN-ComeFrom

Should you really not judge your desires? What about bad things, like desiring to kill someone?

First of all – killing is not a true desire. I know this is an extreme example, but bear with me here. If someone thinks his desire is to "kill someone," his true desire may be:

- To no longer have this person in his life, or
- To have relationships with only supportive people
  (I am guessing at this point that the person he wants to kill is not providing a supportive relationship.)

Killing someone is ONE WAY to weed out the bad apples from your life, sure – but there are other options. There are ALWAYS other options; ones that are not illegal or immoral.

We will learn to explore other options to our desires in a later chapter. Either way, violence and harming another is NEVER a good option to pursue. (DO NOT KILL ANYONE! Look for your deeper desire and pursue that instead.)

> *"The first one to throw a punch losses the argument, as they are proving that they had nothing more intelligent to say."*
> *– Eileen Gutknecht*
> *(My mom, to name one of her many credits.)*

Takeaway: Behind any perceived desire to harm, there is a deeper desire waiting to be discovered; one with solutions that do not involve violence.

As you look for your desires, your want may change from,
I want to kill Person X.
to
I desire to no longer be in contact with Person X.
I desire to be only in relationships that are mutually supportive and fulfilling.
I desire money (I'm thinking the whole "life insurance" scenario here. Again there are other options, besides killing, that would be better to pursue.)

Desire Rule #4 – You must feel comfortable with your desire

While you are searching for your desires, take note if your desire does not feel right and trust that feeling. Examine it a little more. If you go after a desire you are not emotionally comfortable with, you will either never achieve it, or you may obtain it only to lose it.

For instance, getting rich is often something people think they want, but at heart, may not be emotionally ready to handle. Many of us have gotten the message growing up that "money is the root of all evil" and "rich people are greedy." If you have such negative thoughts about money, then gaining financial wealth will continue to be a struggle. [See more about money in the Part 2, Chapter 2 - "You don't really desire money"]

You may also want to add to your desires the desire to feel comfortable with your desire. So, if your desire is to be wealthy you may first have to "desire to feel comfortable with the idea of being wealthy" in order to make your desire a reality or to hold on to wealth when you get it. (A book that might help you get more comfortable in your desire for wealth is *Secrets of the Millionaire Mind* by T. Harv Eker.)

Desiring to first feel comfortable with your desire can be an important first step. You can then make sure you're ready for what you think you want. If you want to lose weight, and your true desire is to feel attractive, ask yourself if you are emotionally ready for that.

Ask yourself, "what ideas go along with my desire to feel attractive?" Perhaps:

- If you felt attractive you would receive more attention? How will that feel? Are you able to handle that attention, or does it scare you?
- You might have more confidence. But ask yourself, if you had more confidence, what do you feel you would you be capable of doing then that you aren't doing now? Are you ready for that? Or is that thing you are envisioning maybe your true desire after all? (I'm guessing it is.)

It may be necessary to desire feeling comfortable with the idea of feeling attractive before you can really begin to pursue feeling attractive.

You must truly be in synch with or excited by your desires, or success will elude you. If you are not emotionally ready to feel "attractive," break your desire down to something that feels more comfortable. Make it something that you can easily imagine. Like, "I desire to find a hairstyle that I love." Work with that until you feel comfortable with the whole experience of feeling attractive.

One clue that you might need to break down your desire into manageable bites is if you cannot imagine what it would be like if you achieved it. Granted, reality will be different from what you imagine, but if you can't picture yourself happily feeling attractive, you will need to either break it down to a more manageable desire or desire to feel comfortable with your desire.

> *"Man's Desires are limited by his Perceptions;*
> *none can desire what he has not perceived."*
> *- William Blake*

Keeping this in mind, your desire may change from:
I desire to lose 25 pounds.
to
I desire to feel confident and attractive.
I desire to love my body.
I desire to find a life partner.
I desire to compete in a marathon.

Takeaway: Make sure you are comfortable with your desire before you pursue it.

SSN– Unanswered Prayers
http://bit.ly/SSN-Unanswered

Side Note: You are already beautiful

Please know that you are beautiful, attractive and lovable just the way you are. I promise you this is true. Beauty is presented in so many different ways. The key to letting other's see your attractiveness is to find your unique beauty and focus on that, not where you feel you are lacking.

Finding and knowing your unique beauty allows the rest of us to see it too. Whether that be your eyes, your sense of humor, your kindness, your laugh, your intelligence, your voice, or whatever makes you uniquely and wonderfully you, that is your beauty. You will often find that when you focus on your unique beauty, your confidence increases and you naturally become more attractive to others. But you need to let your beauty out in order for the rest of us to see and feel it. If your beauty is your voice, sing! If it's your intelligence, tackle tough problems! If it's your sense of humor, crack the joke! If it's your eyes, flash them at people!

And remember, what makes you beautiful may change with time, but you always have something that makes you beautiful, attractive and lovable. The color of our eyes may dull, but the kind words that you say may get kinder and more thoughtful with age.

Let YOUR unique beauty shine!

Find beauty everywhere. When you see it everywhere, people will see it in you. (Though my wish to the world is that 1980s big hair never be considered attractive again!)

"Since the beginning of time never has there been another with my mind, my heart, my eyes, my ears, my hands, my hair, my mouth. None that came before, none that live today, and none that come tomorrow can walk and talk and move and think exactly like me. All men are my brothers yet I am different from each. I am a unique creature."
- Og Mandino, "The Greatest Salesman in the World"

Takeaway: You are unique. You are beautiful. There is beauty in everyone and everything.

(For more on this topic read Part 2, Chapter 1 – "You are worthy of your desires")

Desire Rule #5 – Desires don't have to include EVERYTHING – find the parts and pieces of what you DO desire

Sometimes the all-ness of a desire can encompass too much. Or sometimes the things you think you want are tied up with things you don't want. Sometimes it is best to look at the parts of the want, so you can create desires to fit your unique self.

For instance, the idea of being married brings with it all kinds of connotations. Marriage is a huge concept that means so many different things. We all saw different marriages as we grew up, so we each formed different expectations about what a marriage is supposed to look and feel like.

The idea of getting married scared the crap out of me for a long time. Too many of the examples I saw did NOT look that desirable. Some parts did, but other parts did not seem worth pursuing.

Perhaps, like me, some of the examples of married life you have seen included parts you liked, and parts you did not. Maybe you loved seeing the companionship, but you also saw a lot of marriages where the woman ended up abandoning her dreams to aid her husband's dreams and raise a family. Or, you saw nagging bossy wives who criticized everything their husbands said or did and basically crushed his will to do anything that might upset her. You may not like either of those examples of marriage. Who would? Just because that is what you have seen, that does not mean that your marriage needs to be like that.

Keep the parts that you like and dump the parts you don't want! YOUR relationship can be, function, and look like whatever you choose (and your significant other is in agreement with). It doesn't matter what anyone else's relationship is like. Clarify what you desire, such as "companionship with a loving partner who supports you in the pursuit of your dreams as you support your partner's." Break the mold and be unique! No matter how much your mother's sister looks down at you for "not living according to the rules," I guarantee if you are living your life YOUR way, you will be happier for it.

"You must have control of the authorship of your own destiny. The pen that writes your life story must be held in your own hand."
— Irene C. Kassorla

Keeping this in mind, your desire may change from:
I desire to get married.
to
I desire to create a wonderful life partnership with someone.
I desire to be in a relationship that is mutually supportive.

I desire to have a healthy sex life that is fulfilling to both me and my partner.

Takeaway: Make your desires unique to you. Use others' examples as your testing ground. Take what you like from each of them. Leave what you don't like.

Desire Rule #6 – It's okay if you don't know what you desire

What if you don't know what you want or desire? This has been one of my biggest dilemmas in my search to figure out what I want to "be when I grow up" and what I want out of life. I've always kind of felt like I didn't know what I wanted. So I just followed wherever my interests led. As I followed, watched, learned and listened, I developed more and more ideas about what I did desire. I desired to know what I desired, and bit-by-bit, pieces came to me.

If you're not always sure what you want or desire, I encourage you to explore, read, take a class –do SOMETHING! Follow your natural interests and you'll discover your desires along the way.

Following your natural curiosities can be great desires in and of themselves. Some would argue that they are the only necessary desires. Following your natural curiosities can lead you in amazing unknown directions as long as you stay open to the possibilities. After all, did Bill Gates set out to be one of the richest men in the world, or did he set out wanting to learn more about computers? Look where his interest led him!

Pay attention to the things you DON'T like too. When you know what you don't like, you can use that as a tool to find what you DO like. Identify what you don't like about a situation, then envision the opposite. Is that more appealing to you?

For instance, if you don't like your current job but you're not sure what kind of occupation you want, ask yourself, "What do I like, or not like, about this job?" before deciding what you do desire in a new one. For instance if you are in accounting and don't enjoy sitting at a desk all day staring at numbers, ask yourself, "What is it about this job that I don't like?"

Maybe it's the sitting all day. What about desiring a line of work that allows you to move your body more? Like waitressing? Or doing guided tours of national parks? Or teaching yoga classes? Or being a landscaper? Or a dog walker?

Maybe it's not the sitting that you mind, but all the numbers and formulas. What about becoming a psychologist? Or a designer? Or a customer service agent? Or an airplane pilot?

The possibilities are endless. It is by looking at the opposite of what you don't like that can focus your attention on a whole new world of possibilities. Following your passions and interests and using your dislikes will help you to hone in on what you really desire.

> *"Follow your bliss and the universe will open doors*
> *for you where there were only walls"*
> *— Joseph Campbell*

If you don't know what you want, try exploring these desires:
To know what I desire
To explore my love of _____
To see and experience as many different careers as it takes
to find one that calls to me.
To notice when I am having fun and really enjoying myself.

Takeaway: It's okay to desire to know what your desires are and explore that.

Okay, so now let's get even closer to our desires...

Unscribbling Exercise 3 –

What's your motivation? What do you really want?

Lets look at those five goals you came up with earlier, and get to the heart of them. What are you REALLY trying to accomplish by obtaining these wants? To steal a line from our acting friends, "What's your motivation?" In analyzing your goal/want, focus on what you really desire for your life.

Within each of your five goals, look for your true desires. To help you find what you really desire, ask your self:

- Why do I want this?
- What feeling or experience would I gain from this?
- Is it really me that wants this, or someone else?
- What will my life look and feel like once I have this?
- How will my life change once I have this?
- What will I be able to do/have/be if I accomplish this?
- What new goal would I set if I met this?
- Why is this important to me?
- If I did this, what will I be able to do that I cannot do now?
- If I could not accomplish this, is there something else I would want?

Let's look at our examples to get started. For now, let's leave your "buts" out of it. Instead, let's take your want and add, "I want this because I desire..." and fill in the blank.

Don't censor yourself here. Write down anything and everything that comes to mind. We will work on clarifying your desires next. For now we just want to get your thoughts flowing.

P.S. It may be helpful to get a friend to help you through this section, or submit your wants to us and we can offer some possibilities at www.unscribbling.com.

Lets take a look at our sample wants and identify the desire behind our wants.

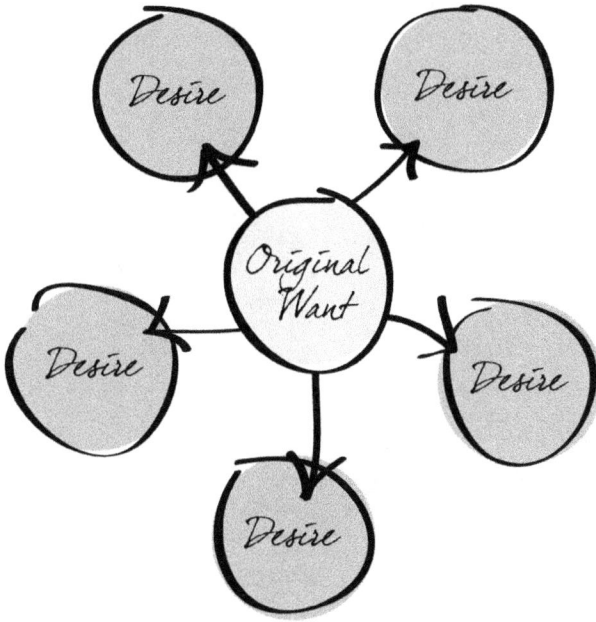

1. I want to own my own home.
Ask: Why do you want to own your own home?

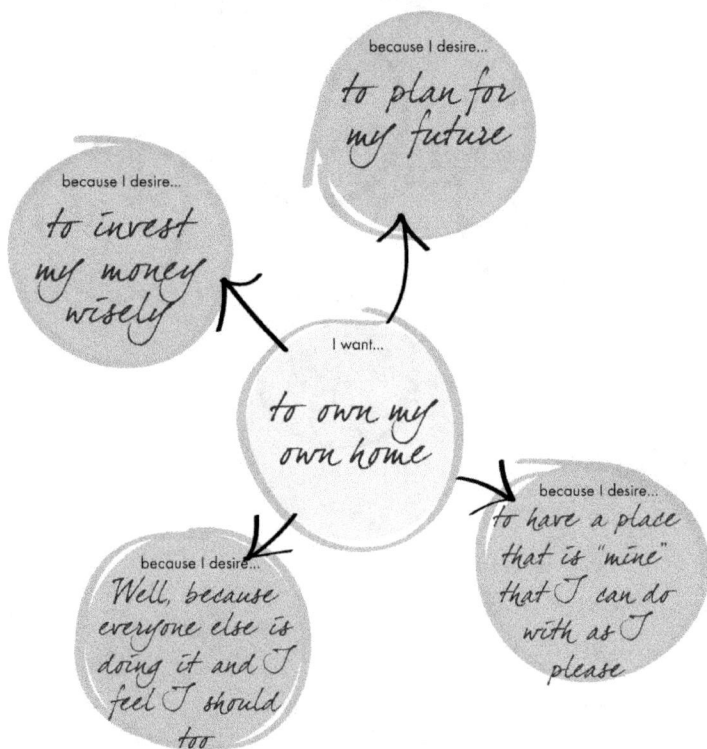

because I desire...

to plan for my future

because I desire...

to invest my money wisely

I want...

to own my own home

because I desire...

to have a place that is "mine" that I can do with as I please

because I desire...

Well, because everyone else is doing it and I feel I should too

2.   I want to be in a romantic relationship.

Ask: Why do you want to be in a romantic relationship?

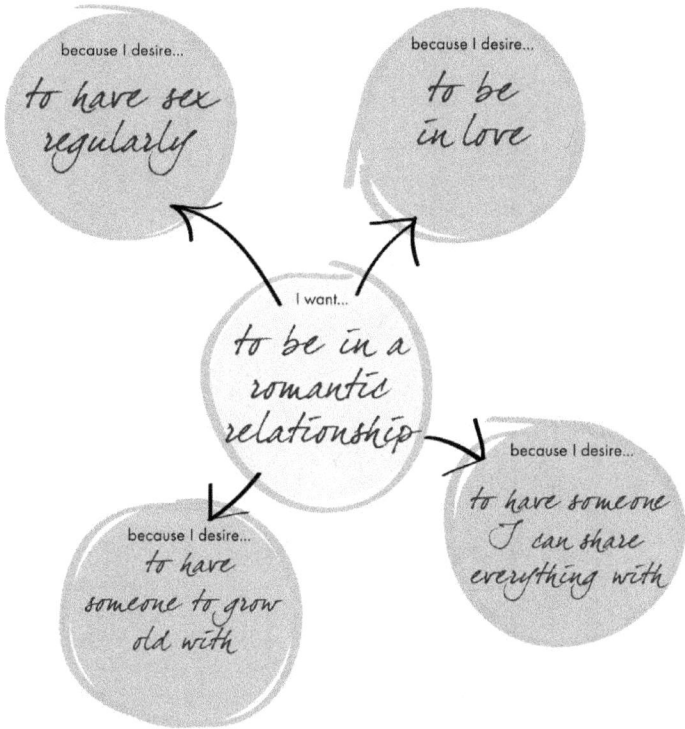

because I desire...

to have sex regularly

because I desire...

to be in love

I want...

to be in a romantic relationship

because I desire...

to have someone to grow old with

because I desire...

to have someone I can share everything with

3. I want a job that pays well.
Ask: Why do you want a job that pays well?

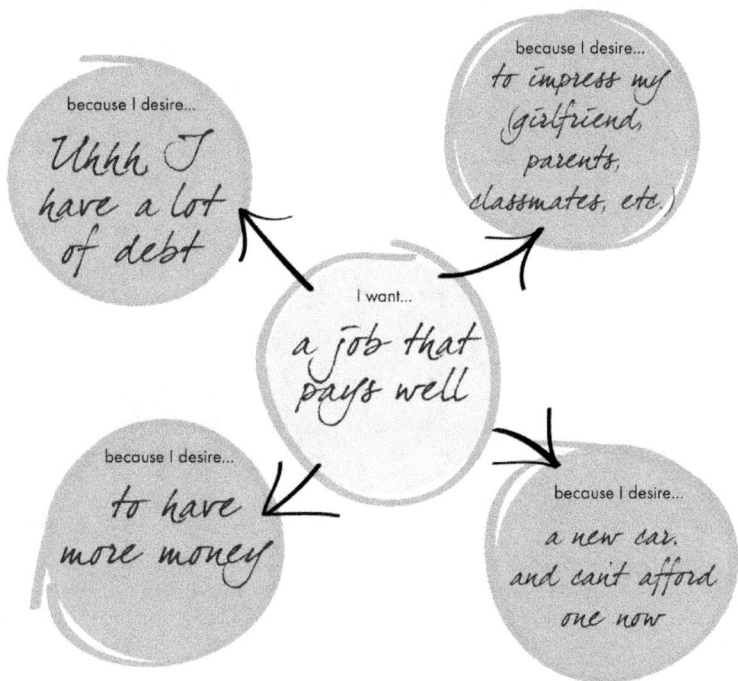

because I desire...
Uhhh I have a lot of debt

because I desire...
to impress my (girlfriend, parents, classmates, etc.)

I want...
a job that pays well

because I desire...
to have more money

because I desire...
a new car and can't afford one now

4. I want to lose weight.

Ask: Why do you want to lose weight?

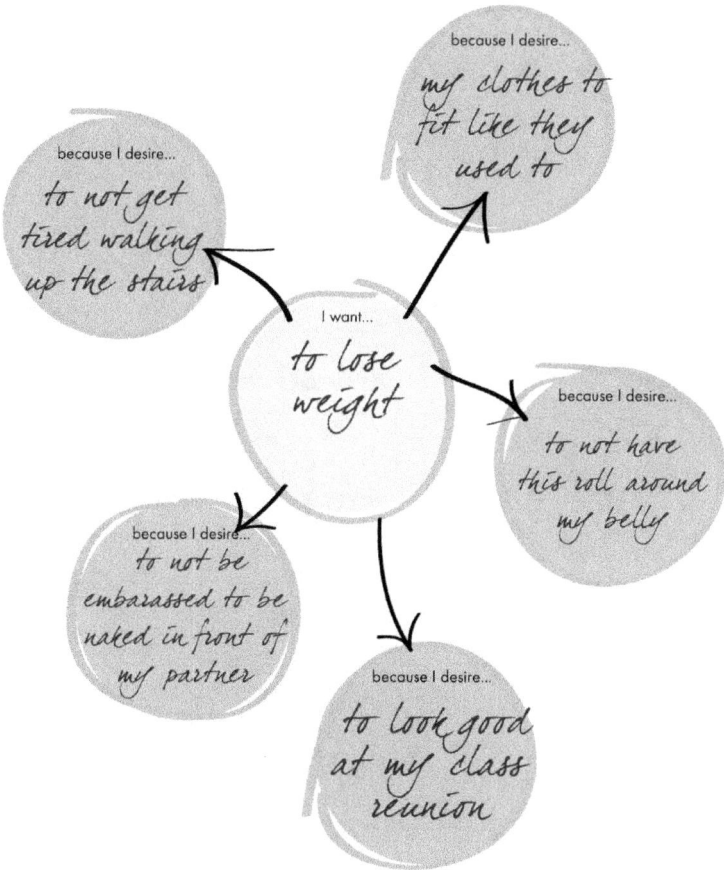

because I desire...
my clothes to fit like they used to

because I desire...
to not get tired walking up the stairs

I want...
to lose weight

because I desire...
to not have this roll around my belly

because I desire...
to not be embarassed to be naked in front of my partner

because I desire...
to look good at my class reunion

5. I want a baby.
Ask: Why do you want a baby?

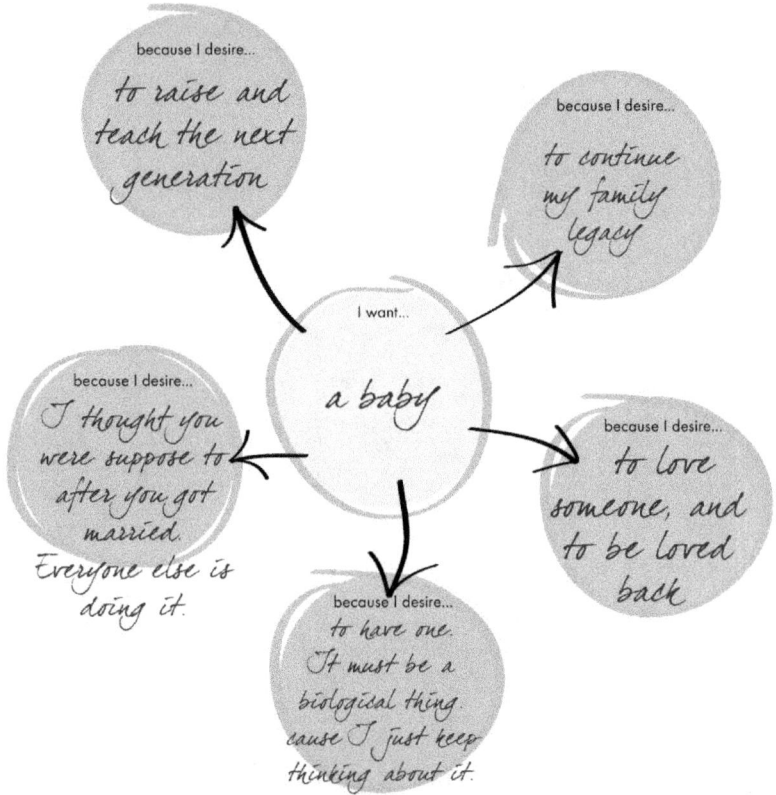

because I desire...
to raise and teach the next generation

because I desire...
to continue my family legacy

I want...

a baby

because I desire...
I thought you were suppose to after you got married. Everyone else is doing it.

because I desire...
to love someone, and to be loved back

because I desire...
to have one. It must be a biological thing. cause I just keep thinking about it.

6. I want to be a billionaire.
Ask: Why do you want to be a billionaire?

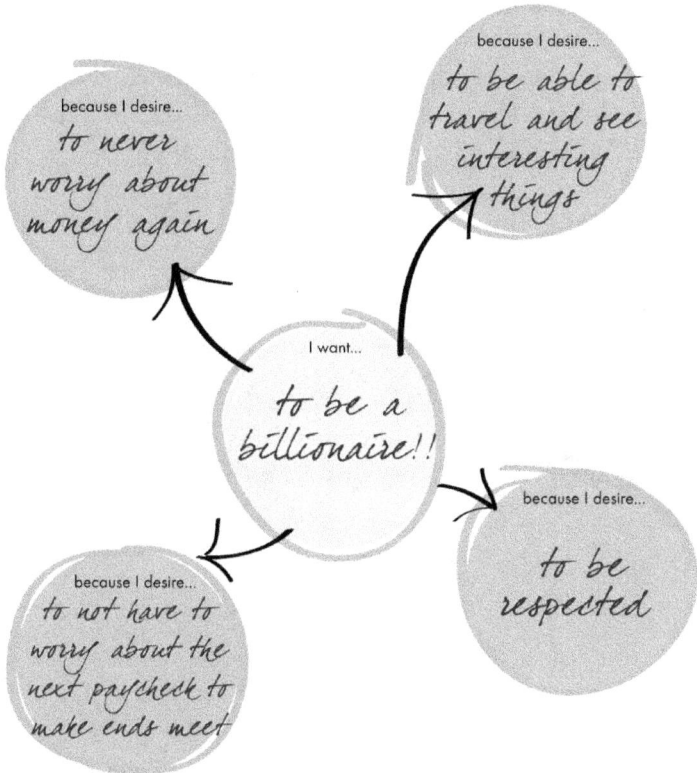

because I desire...
to never worry about money again

because I desire...
to be able to travel and see interesting things

I want...
to be a billionaire!!

because I desire...
to be respected

because I desire...
to not have to worry about the next paycheck to make ends meet

Your Turn...

Questions to ask yourself to get to the heart of your desires:

- Why do I want this?
- What feeling or experience would I gain from this?
- Is it really me that wants this, or someone else?
- What will my life look and feel like once I have this?
- How will my life change once I have this?
- What will I be able to do/have/be if I accomplish this?
- What new goal would I set if I met this?
- Why is this important to me?
- If I did this, what will I be able to do that I cannot do now?
- If I could not accomplish this, is there something else I would want?

EXTRAS
Download a copy of this worksheet at:
http://www.unscribbling.com/extras

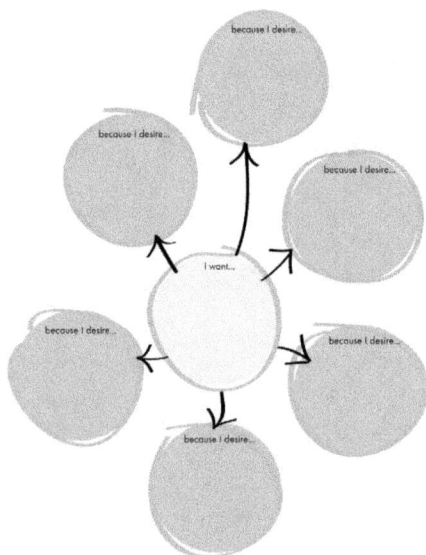

Now let's look at your "but" and get you "butless"

In Exercise 1, you listed your wants followed by your buts as to why you are having a hard time achieving your want. Our examples included:

1. I want to own my own home,
but I don't have enough money.
2. I want to be in a relationship,
but I don't have time to date.
3. I want a job that pays well,
but I would have to go back to school to get one.
4. I want to lose weight,
but I don't have time to work out.
5. I want a baby,
but I can't seem to get pregnant.
6. I want to be a billionaire,
but I only make $35,000 a year.

Hidden in your but is another desire. Flip the negative part of the statement into a positive to find the hidden desire. For example:

1. but I don't have enough money.
I desire more money.
2. but I don't have time to date.
I desire more free time away from responsibilities.
3. but I would have to go back to school to get [a better job].
I desire to be qualified for a better job.
4. but I don't have time to work out.
I desire to have a work out I can fit in my schedule.
5. but I can't seem to get pregnant.
I desire to get pregnant.
6. but I only make $35,000 a year.
I desire more money.

Add your new desires to the answers you came up with in Exercise 3.

SSN– He would not give up his "buts"
http://bit.ly/SSN-Buts

You're not done yet. I warned you this was the tough step…

Sometimes you have to dig a little deeper into your desires to get to the true core desires.

It's important to dig deep enough so you are solving the correct problem, and that you are pursuing your true desire. Sometimes the initial desires that you come up with are like your original "want" and they don't quite go deep enough into the heart of your desire. Sometimes they do. It's knowing when you've gone far enough that can be tricky.

There are three general rules of thumb for how to know if you have dug deep enough into your desires. They are:

1. Is it a feeling or an experience you would like to have?
2. Can you write your desire in the form of a question?
3. Does it feel right to you?

When you can say yes to all three, you're ready to move on to the next step. Let's look at each of these in turn.

Is it a feeling or an experience you'd like to have?

Your desires generally come down to feelings or experiences you want to have, because life is basically feeling and experiencing. Ask yourself with each desire you came up with, "What do I want to feel or experience with this?"

As with our original want of "a job that pays well," one of the possible desires we came up with was "to impress my girlfriend, parents, classmates, etc." But what is the feeling or experience behind that possible desire? Could it be, "To be proud of myself and feel confident in who I am?" That is a feeling, and probably much closer to the heart of the desires.

Keep digging into your desires until you get to an experience or feeling. That is the true heart of your desire(s).

It all goes back to what feeling or experience you want, or, in the case of business, that you want to provide someone else when they interact with you. If the desires you came up with are not feelings or experiences, dig a little deeper.

"A true desire is not to have but to be. We are all creatures in poten-tial, and the true purpose of desire is to unfold that wholeness, to become what we can be."
– Eric Butterworth, Spiritual Economics

Takeaway: Look for the feeling or experience you are looking for in each desire.

SSN– A True Desire is Not to HAVE but to BE
http://bit.ly/SSN-ToBe

Side Note: Businesses provide feelings and experiences

If you are identifying your business' desires, explore the feelings and experiences you want to provide your clients and customers. Work of any kind is a venue where you get to use your talents to help make OTHER people's dreams and desires come true. (Hopefully yours too, in the process.) You are not working to change anyone, rather to provide a feeling or experience that they are looking for with your services or products. So you may want to ask yourself, what feelings or experiences does my business desire to provide through my products or services?

Just like we have options to fulfill our dreams, our clients have options as to whose services they choose. Your clients and customers are working with your business or your product based on the experience, as well as the service, you are providing them. They could go elsewhere, but there is something about the experience you provide that makes them want to work with you. For instance, depending on the experience you are looking for, you can decide to stay at the Four Seasons or Motel 6. Both provide a place to sleep, but they create very different experiences. So what feeling or experience are your clients getting or expecting from your business?

If you are an employee, you too are helping to fulfill the desires of others; the desires of the company you work for, as well as the desires of your company's clients and customers. Ask yourself, what experience are you providing your employers? Remember they get to choose who works for them. Your personal brand of service is as important as your company's brand of service if you want to keep your job or get promoted. Remember to be thinking about your personal brand as you perform your duties, for you are providing a service with an experience too.

> *"The best way to find yourself is to lose yourself in*
> *the service of others."*
> *- Gandhi*

Takeaway: Businesses and employees are helping make other's dreams come true. Clients will choose to work with you (or not) based on the experience you provide them – not merely based on the service or product you provide.

Can you write your desire in the form of a question?

If you can't fit your desire into a question, you may need to dig a bit deeper. In the case of the art center, the question became, "How can we display art?" That works. That is something you can explore.

One of the possible desires we came up with for wanting to own your own home was, "because everyone else is doing it and I feel I should too." In this case, you still really don't know what to solve for. How do you solve for "because everyone else is doing it?"

Try putting your desire in the form of a question. Such as:

How can I (or we) _____?
What ways are there to _____?

If you can't yet form a question, go back and ask yourself the questions from Exercise 3:

- Why do I want this?
- What feeling or experience would I gain from this?
- Is it really me that wants this, or someone else?
- What will my life look and feel like once I have this?
- How will my life change once I have this?
- What will I be able to do/have/be if I accomplish this?
- What new goal would I set if I met this?
- Why is this important to me?
- If I did this, what will I be able to do that I cannot do now?
- If I could not accomplish this, is there something else I would want?

So let's look at possible desires behind "because everyone else is doing it." If you keep digging you may find out that you want to "do what everyone else is doing" because:

- I will feel accepted and like I belong.
- I want to feel comfortable with my peers.
- I want to feel respected.

Try these answers in the form of a question:

- How can I feel accepted and like I belong?

- How can I feel comfortable with my peers?
- How can I feel respected?

If you can turn it into a question, you are ready to go to the next step and start exploring!

"One who asks a question is a fool for five minutes; one who does not ask a question remains a fool forever."
—Chinese Proverb

Takeaway: Be sure you can put your desire into the form of a question before you move on.

Does it feel right to you?

Your emotions will tell you if you're ready to move on. Diving into your wants to identify the feelings and experiences you desire can be very revealing, and because of that, often very emotional. Emotions can help you pinpoint what is truly important to you. When you list a possible desire if you feel either a lightening of the heart, a sudden urge to cry, a rush of guilt or a hesitation to write it down – pay attention!! Your emotions are trying to tell you which way to go.

The bottom line is to trust your gut (or your heart). Ask yourself, "Is this truly what I desire?" and then listen. If you are not a "gut" person, or you did not feel any particular emotion, contemplate your list and identify which desires from the list logically seem most true to you.

With the Art Center project, we really did desire a way to display art. We felt we had dug deep enough in the desire to move on to the next step of setting our intentions and brainstorming. But that was our "designer" guts talking.

If we were the investors, I might have dug a little deeper and asked, "Why do we want a way to display art?" Possible answers include:

• to educate the public on Native American Art
• to create an income generator (sales)

Depending on the investor's gut, they may pursue either, both, or some other desire. But it is up to the individual to know when to move on to the next step.

As always, make the desire something that feels right and resonate with YOU.

"Think wrongly, if you please, but in all cases think for yourself."
— Doris Lessing

Takeaway: Pursue the desires that resonate with you and feel right.

Side Note: Hierarchy of Needs

If we wanted to, we could take each of these new desires and go back even further. And if we really want to psychoanalyze, we could probably boil everything down to Maslow's Hierarchy of needs. However, I have found that going to the point where you can put your desire in the form of a question, and find the feeling or experience and/or it feels right to you, that will be far enough.

Maslow's Hierarchy as shown on: http://en.wikipedia. org/wiki/Maslow's_hierarchy_of_needs

SSN– The "Need" to Know God (SSN)
http://bit.ly/SSN-KnowGod

Take each desire and make sure we have found the feeling or experience we truly desire.

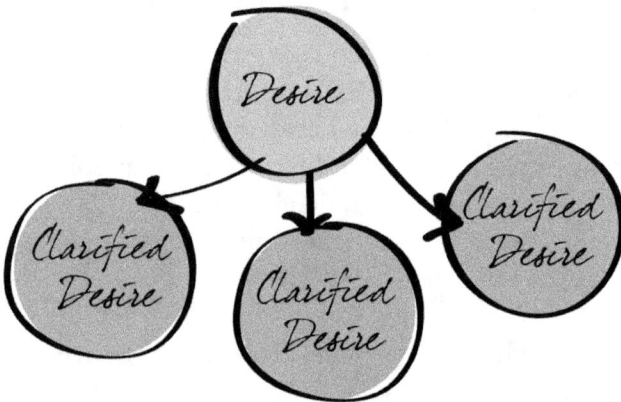

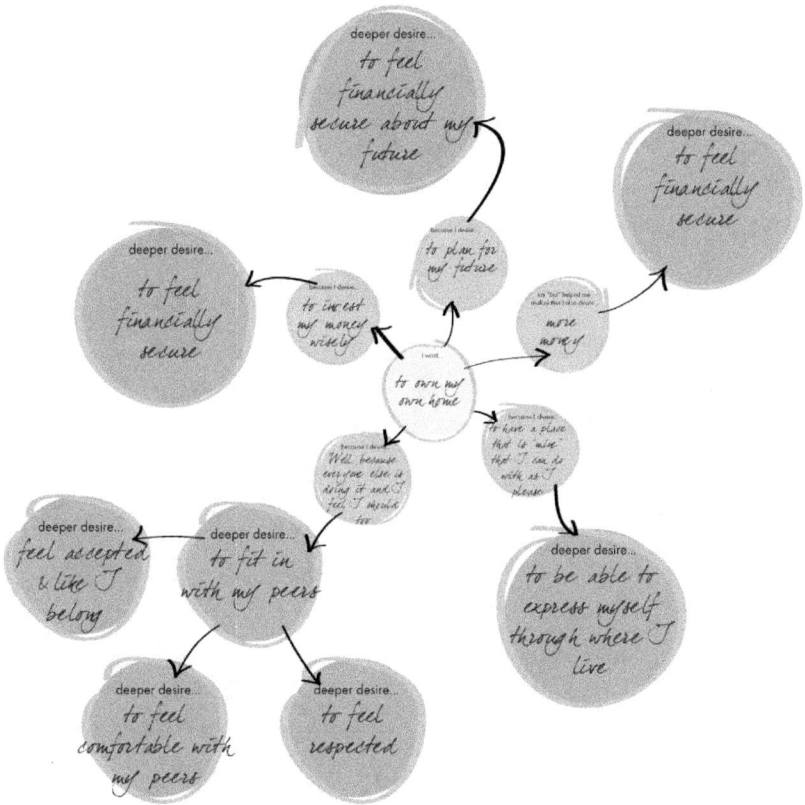

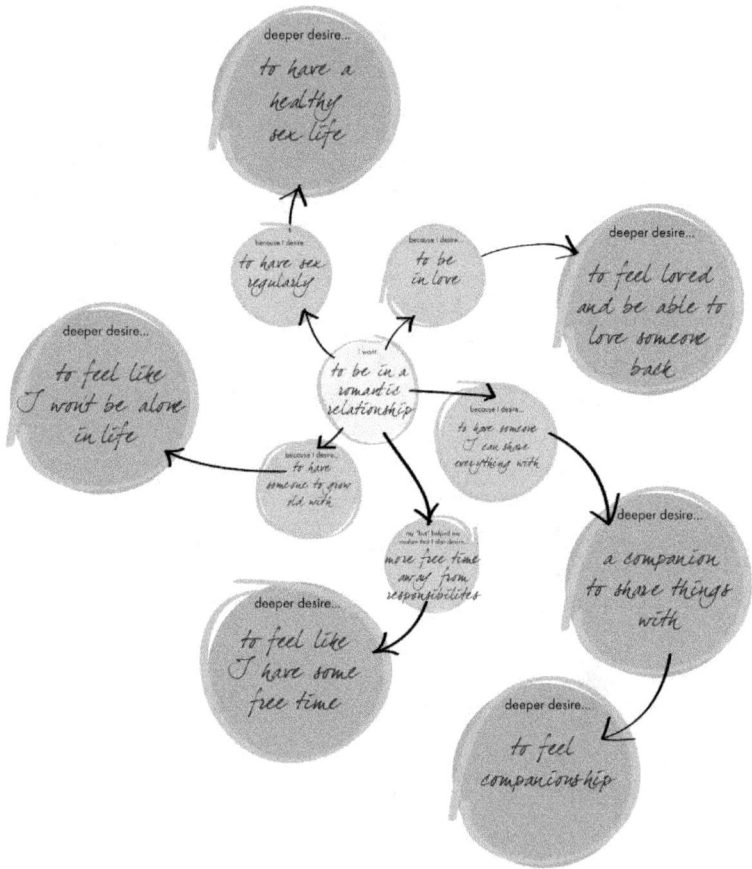

deeper desire...

to have a
healthy
sex life

because I desire
to have sex
regularly

because I desire
to be
in love

deeper desire...

to feel loved
and be able to
love someone
back

deeper desire...

to feel like
I wont be alone
in life

I want
to be in a
romantic
relationship

because I desire...
to have someone
I can share
everything with

because I desire...
to have
someone to grow
old with

deeper desire...

a companion
to share things
with

my "but" helped me
realise that I also desire...
more free time
away from
responsibilities

deeper desire...

to feel like
I have some
free time

deeper desire...

to feel
companionship

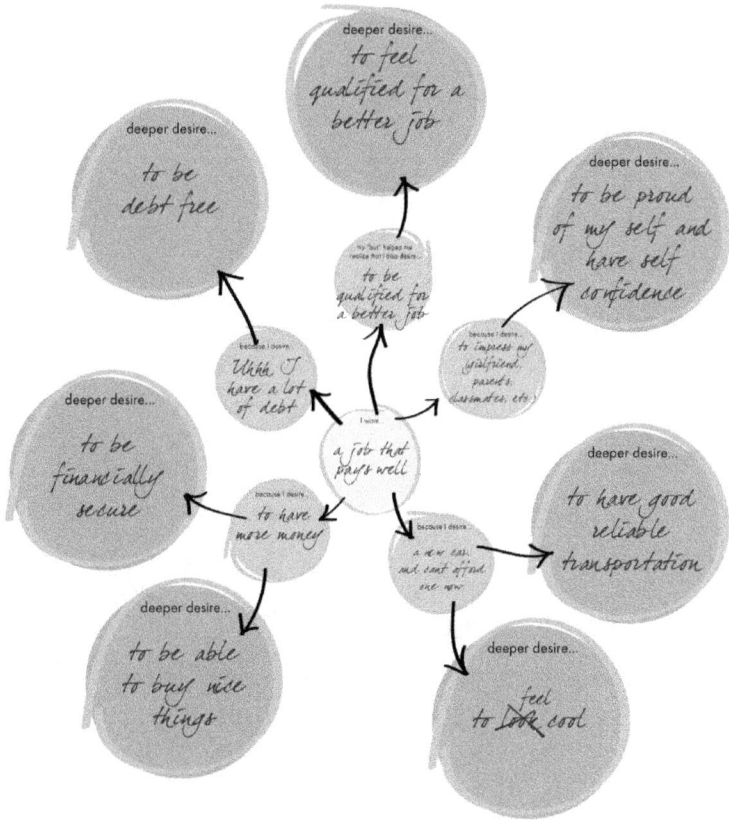

deeper desire...
to feel
qualified for a
better job

deeper desire...
to be
debt free

deeper desire...
to be proud
of my self and
have self
confidence

my "but" helped me
realize that this desire...
to be
qualified for
a better job

because I desire...
Uhhh I
have a lot
of debt

because I desire...
to impress my
girlfriend,
parents,
classmates, etc.

I want...
a job that
pays well

deeper desire...
to be
financially
secure

because I desire...
to have
more money

because I desire...
a new car
and cant afford
one now

deeper desire...
to have good
reliable
transportation

deeper desire...
to be able
to buy nice
things

deeper desire...
to ~~look~~ feel cool

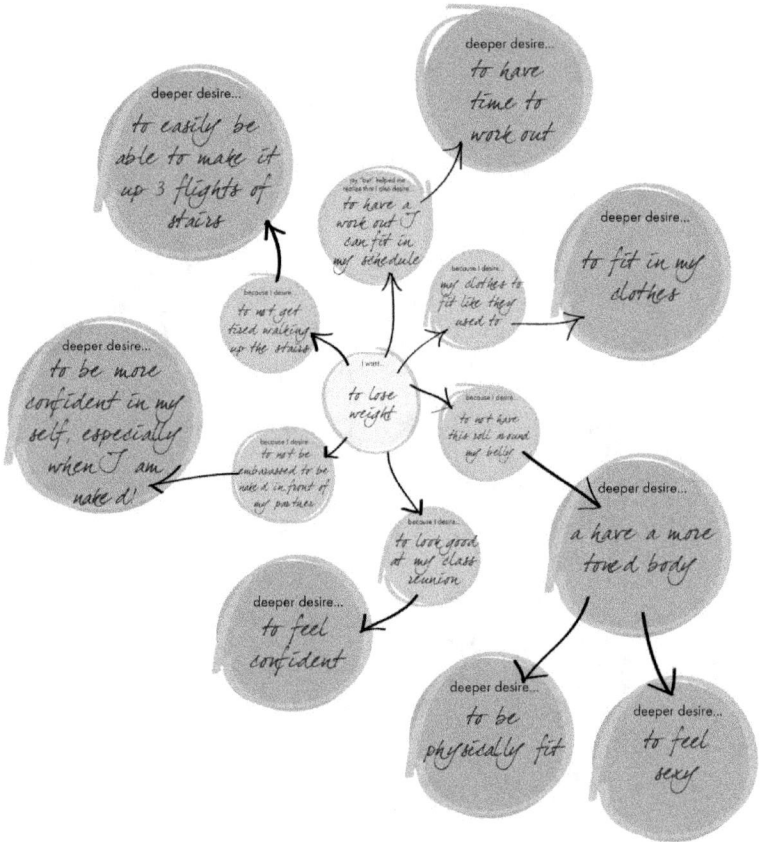

deeper desire...
to have time to work out

deeper desire...
to easily be able to make it up 3 flights of stairs

deeper desire...
to fit in my clothes

deeper desire...
to be more confident in my self, especially when I am naked

deeper desire...
a have a more toned body

deeper desire...
to feel confident

deeper desire...
to be physically fit

deeper desire...
to feel sexy

I want...
to lose weight

because I desire
to not get tired walking up the stairs

my "but" helped me realize that I also desire
to have a work out I can fit in my schedule

because I desire
my clothes to fit like they used to

because I desire
to not have this roll around my belly

because I desire
to not be embarrassed to be naked in front of my partner

because I desire
to look good at my class reunion

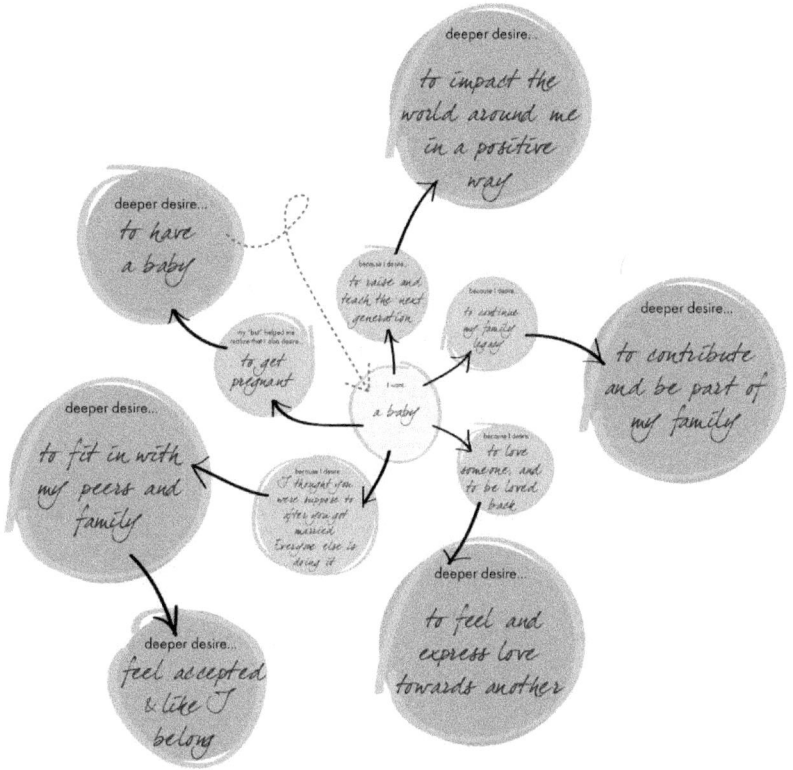

deeper desire...
to impact the world around me in a positive way

deeper desire...
to have a baby

because I desire...
to raise and teach the next generation

because I desire...
to continue my family legacy

deeper desire...
to contribute and be part of my family

my "but" helped me realise that I also desire...
to get pregnant

I want...
a baby

deeper desire...
to fit in with my peers and family

because I desire...
I thought you were suppose to often even get married. Everyone else is doing it

because I desire...
to love someone, and to be loved back

deeper desire...
to feel and express love towards another

deeper desire...
feel accepted & like I belong

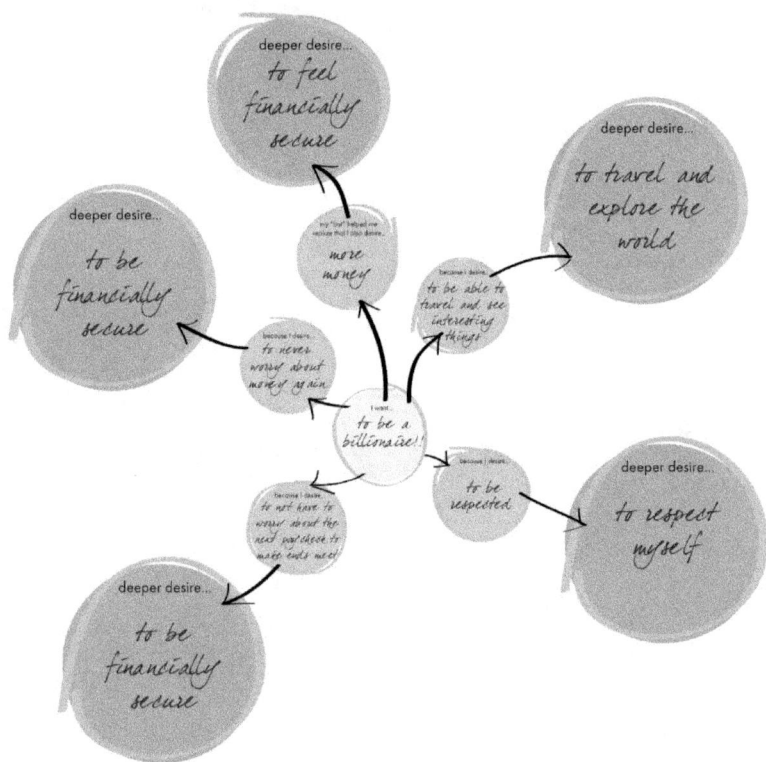

deeper desire...
to feel
financially
secure

deeper desire...
to travel and
explore the
world

deeper desire...
to be
financially
secure

my "list" helped me
realize that I also desire...
more
money

because I desire...
to be able to
travel and see
interesting
things

because I desire...
to never
worry about
money again

I want...
to be a
billionaire!!

because I desire...
to be
respected

because I desire...
to not have to
worry about the
next purchase to
make ends meet

deeper desire...
to respect
myself

deeper desire...
to be
financially
secure

Exercise 4 - Now it's your turn! Clarify your personal desires

Keep digging into your desires until you can:
1. Identify a feeling or an experience you would like to have.
2. Turn the desire into a question.
3. Feel like the desire fits right with you.

EXTRAS
Download a copy of this worksheet at:
http://www.unscribbling.com/extras

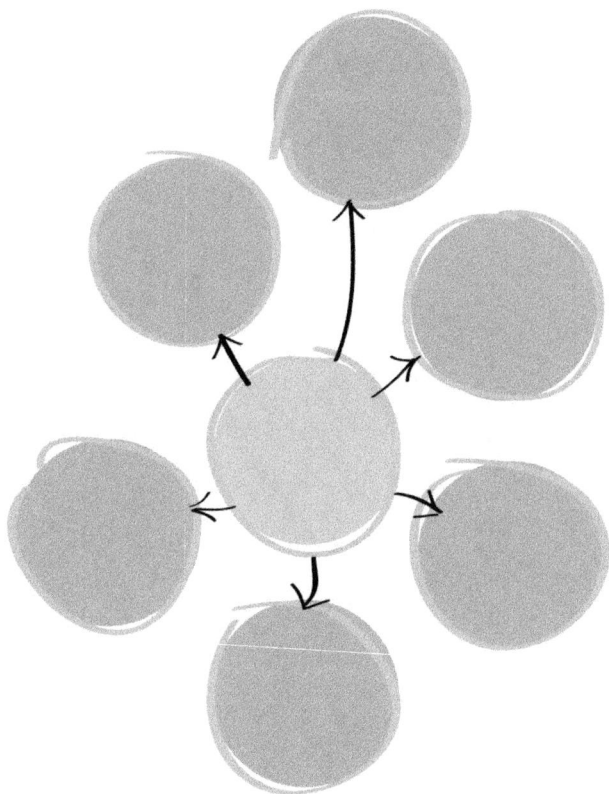

Step 2 – Intend

Once you become aware of what your true desire is, you can now set your intentions, objectives, commander's intent, compass point or whatever you want to call it. (Just don't use the "goal" word please. Remember, goals and wants tend to be defined solutions, not the desire behind the solution.)

Why change from desiring something to intending it?

When you think of a desire, your thoughts are focused on the idea that you lack what you desire. "I don't have ____, but I desire it." This is not mentality empowering. On the other hand, when you think of an intention you set your thoughts toward achievement. It is a subtle distinction, but one that can make a strong difference in your thought patterns.

Say out loud:
I desire to be financially secure.

Now try:
I intend to be financially secure.

Did you feel the difference? Intending is coming from an empowered point in you. When you intend something you are declaring that one day you will get there.

This step helps to transform a problem/struggle/lack into something you can get excited about, because you clearly see where you intend to one day be and you know you have the ability to get there. This step opens your mind to what your life could look like once your intention is realized.

Now when you see financially secure people, you aren't looking at them from a point of jealousy, rather from a point that says, "Oh yeah, baby, I'll see you there in a jiffy! I can't wait until we are sharing a syrah dock side discussing how bright the future is going to be!"

Once you set your intention, you also set your excitement. This excitement can help spur you on to take action.

You can achieve your desires, so empower yourself and intend it!

> *"Each decision we make, each action we take,*
> *is born out of an intention."*
> *- Sharon Salzberg*

Takeaway: Turn your desire into an intention to empower yourself and excite your mind towards fulfilling your intentions.

Exercise 5 - Let's turn our example desires into intentions:

You may have noticed that as you investigated each of your original wants, and drilled down to the true desires, a lot of your desires are listed under more than one want. That is perfectly normal. At this point, your original wants no longer matter; it's the true desires that are important. Take whatever desires appeared and turn them into intentions.

For example:

- I intend to feel financially secure.
- I intend to be able to express myself through where I live.
- I intend to feel respected.
- I intend to have a healthy sex life.
- I intend to have companionship.
- I intend to have some free time.
- I intend to know I won't be alone in life.
- I intend to have good reliable transportation.
- I intend to be debt free.
- I intend to fit into my clothes.
- I intend to feel sexy.
- I intend to be confident.
    - I intend to impact the world around me in a positive way.
    - I intend to contribute and be part of my family.
    - I intend to travel and explore the world.

After you write down your intentions, ask yourself, "does this feel right for me?" If not, keep exploring.

It's an easy, but powerful step.

Step 3 – Brainstorm (Question)

Now that you know what you are intending to create in your life, you can start to explore possible ways to fulfill those intentions. This is the part of the process that people typically think of when they do problem solving. It's the part that involves finding possible solutions – the brainstorming. But there is a little more to the unscribbling process than just brainstorming possibilities. I actually want you to NOT think about the possibilities in order to find them. Confused? Keep reading, it will all sort itself out.

Start with a question

The first thing you need to do is change your intentions into the form of a question. For instance, if you intend to feel financially secure, you could change that to, "How can I feel financially secure?" After you turn your intention into a question, you can do an initial brain dump of possible solutions right away if you want, but that is actually NOT the point of putting your desire into a question. And no, you are not on Jeopardy either.

Changing your intentions to questions allows your brain to shift yet again – this time into search mode. You actually don't need to come up with your perfect solution right now. You are just getting your brain ready to look for solutions.

Putting your mind in the search mode allows it to look for possibilities you might not think of in your initial brainstorming of solutions. The best solutions usually need to be processed out of us, as they come to you later, after our brains have had time to think about it.

It's kind of like trying to remember a name. Think about how often a name you were trying to remember comes to you in the shower, or right before you fall asleep – not at the moment you were trying to recall the name. You asked your brain what the name was, it could not connect the neurons immediately, but after you gave it time to look for the answer it found the name. It's your brain's natural process.

When you're trying to remember something, how often do you think, "Oh, it will come to me later." In these instances you trust the processing of our brain. Apply that same approach to imagining all of the ways you can solve your problems and fulfill your desires. By switching intentions into questions, you are switching your brain into search mode and allowing it to do what comes naturally – processing, searching and responding to your request. It could be to recall a name or find the best way for you to feel financially secure.

When you ask your brain a question, it's like you send a message to a little worker bee in our mind with a periscope. The little worker bee is called into action keeping an eye out for good solutions to fulfill the desire. But the worker bee needs its marching orders. Switching intentions into question form is the process of sending the bee/your subconscious its orders. It tells the bee what to look for and bring to your attention. It is part of your brain's natural processing that allows you to go about your day while it stays on the job looking for answers for you. Even when you are watching TV or sleeping, your little bee is looking for anything that might provide an answer to your question. When it finds possible answers, the bee sends the message to your conscious awareness!

The question tells your little bee to be on the lookout for something. Where before you were thinking, "I intend to feel financially secure." Your bee is like, "Okay, that sounds cool to us too." Now you say to the bee, "How do I feel and what things can I do to feel financially secure?" Now your little bee is like, "Oh, dude, this is awesome, let me get to work finding all the ways we can do this and get back to you." Your little bee lives for this stuff! So put the bee to work!

Whenever my clients have big projects coming up, I always ask them to tell me a little bit about the project before they are 100 percent ready to hand it off to me. This allows my brain to start incubating possible solutions and be more ready to proceed when they are ready. Without fail, this always helps the process. Once they are ready, my brain has actually already sent me some options and is still on the lookout for more.

So flip your intentions into a question and put your little bee/ subconscious to work.

> *"A prudent question is one half of wisdom."*
> *– Francis Bacon*

Takeaway: Turn your intention into a question to put your mind to work searching for solutions.

Let's flip some of our examples, from:
- I intend to feel financially secure. Becomes:
  How can I feel financially secure?
- I intend to be able to express myself through where I live. Becomes:
  How can I be able to express myself through where I live?
- I intend to feel respected. Becomes:
  How can I feel respected?
- I intend to have a healthy sex life. Becomes:
  How can I have a healthy sex life?
- I intend to have companionship. Becomes:
  What ways are there to feel companionship?
- I intend to have some free time. Becomes:
  How can I create more free time?
- I intend to feel like I won't be alone in life. Becomes:
  How can I feel companionship?

(That's really what not being alone is about right? When you see things like that, feel free to change them. It's YOUR life. Search for the answers you desire!)

- I intend to have good reliable transportation. Becomes:
  What ways are there to have good, reliable transportation?
- I intend to be debt free. Becomes:
  How can I get free of debt?
- I intend to fit into my clothes. Becomes:
  How can I fit into my clothes?
- I intend to feel sexy. Becomes:
  How can I feel sexy?
- I intend to be confident. Becomes:
  How can I feel more confident?
- I intend to impact the world around me in a positive way. Becomes:
  What ways are there to impact the world around me in a positive way?
- I intend to contribute and be part of my family. Becomes:
  How can I contribute and be part of my family?
- I intend to travel and explore the world. Becomes:
  How can I travel and explore the world?

Okay, I think you get the point.

SSN–Ask the Question
http://bit.ly/SSN-Ask

Be patient and stay open to solutions

Remember, the best solutions don't always come right away. Be patient and give the bee time to work!

Not only is the bee trying to reconnect the neurons in your

brain to remember the possible solutions you have already encountered in life, it's also on the lookout for new solutions. It's sorting through all of the noise of your life and looking for solutions all the time, even when you're not conscious that it is doing so. It stays on the job until you are satisfied.

It's like when you are walking through a department store, on your way to pick up dog treats, and suddenly you stop and do a double take. You're not sure what you saw, but you saw something. Then you realize that you are looking at a toaster. Last week you were thinking, "Gosh, I wish I had a way to toast bread." Your conscious mind had forgotten that you wanted this, but your bee didn't! As you were walking past thousands of items in the store, your bee zeroed in on a solution for you and sent you an alert.

The same thing can happen with any of your intentions. You may intend "to impact the world in a positive way," and then you'll notice a sign about volunteering in your area for Earth Day. You may intend "to create more free time for yourself," when you spot an ad in the newspaper for a new cleaning service offering a half price special, and you can now free up time by having someone else clean the house. You may intend "to find a companion," when you notice the local dog shelter has a dog that might be perfect for you. You've perhaps walked by that sign, or seen that ad, or driven by the shelter ten times before, but your bee wasn't on the job. Now your bee is tuned in to look for solutions and letting you know about them.

So be patient, and stay open to the alerts that the bee is sending. Keep your question in mind and as you find new solutions, keep yourself open by asking, "What else is possible?" This will keep your bee on the job and at full attention.

"Serendipity. Look for something, find something else, and realize that what you've found is more suited to your needs than what you thought you were looking for."
— Lawrence Block

Takeaway: Be patient with your bee, be patient with yourself, and stay open to new possible solutions that come your way.

SSN– The Power of Patience
http://bit.ly/SSN-Patience

Help the Bee!

Sometimes your bee needs to see and experience a few more things in order to come up with good solutions. You can help your bee in this process by exploring, imagining, learning, talking to others and reading more about whatever you sent your bee to look for. Exposure to more things and ways of thinking about things will greatly speed up the process of uncovering possible solutions to fulfilling your desires.

In addition to learning more about what you sent your bee inquiring about, you may also want to help the bee to think differently in order to find possible new solutions. Play brainstorming games, like the "What would _____ do with this intention?" game, but filling in the blank with a whole slew of possible characters:
  • Your wild party girlfriend
  • Apple Computers
  • The President
  • An artist
  • Your spouse
  • Yes, Jesus, too! (Along with the Budda and the Dalai Lama, just to cover all your bases.)

Keep going. The more extreme the entity the better! What would happen if YOU did what you think they would do? Oh, can you imagine the possibilities?

The more knowledge you have about a subject, and the more you have looked at the solution in various ways, the faster the bee can come up with solutions that feel right to you.

*"When you've exhausted all possibilities, remember this —
you haven't."*
— Robert H. Schuller

Takeaway: Help the "bee" (or yourself) by learning more about whatever you are interested in, and explore other ways to look at the problem or desire. It will help you find more possibilities.

P.S. If you are extremely limited on time for problem solving, spend some time thinking about your questions, then take a 20 minute nap or meditate, then do your brainstorming. Give your subconscious brain at least 20 minutes to do its job, distraction free, before you really engage your conscious mind with possible solutions.

Side Note: Stir up the bee with gratitude

Another game that can help you get the bee jacked up and on the job is to list ways that you have already accomplished what you are trying to do. Then say, "Thank you!"

Saying "Thank you" shifts your brain again. It acknowledges that it is possible to meet your intentions by proving that you have already done so. It helps your brain gain confidence in your ability to succeed.

So change the question to: "Where and in what ways am I already _____?"

For instance, "Where and in what ways am I already financially secure?"

Possible answers and thank you statements:
• I do have a job, and I know that my employer will pay me each pay period.
  Thank you for providing a regular paycheck.

- If I had to, I could probably get a loan from my parents.

  Thank you for being a safety net if I really need it.
- If I had to, I could go on unemployment for a while, or food stamps are available.

  Thank you for providing government services if I really need them.
- I could get a roommate or move in with my sister for a while to save on housing costs.

  Thank you for letting me see that I have options to my living situation.
- I could sell some of my investments or furniture.

  Thank me for investing and accumulating things that others will find valuable.
- You know, I am a good worker and would be good at anything I put my mind to. It may not be my dream job, but I can find a job doing something to earn money.

  Thank you for giving me a mind I can apply and use.

Feeling more financially secure yet? If so, rephrase your question again to:

Thank you for all of the wonderful ways I am already financially secure. What other ways can we come up with to increase this feeling of gratitude for my financial security?

Now put the bee to work again. Wow, did you feel that shift?

"Be thankful for what you have; you'll end up having more. If you concentrate on what you don't have, you will never, ever have enough."
–Oprah Winfrey

Takeaway: Shifting into thankfulness will help you find even more to be thankful about.

When do you stop looking for possibilities?

Stay with the process until your intentions are realized. "What? Huh? How do I get anything done?" you ask... When you feel in your gut that you have imagined a possible way to fulfill your desires that works for you, move on to the next steps, BUT always stay in the process of looking, as you never know when a BETTER solution will come along. (Your bee is still working.)

Plus, things can come up while you are exploring solutions that put you on sidetracks and detours, so you have to be ready to zig and zag as necessary in order to stay on the path to fulfilling your intentions. Keep your question of how to reach your intention in your bee's focus and you will NEVER be completely stopped if your plans get sidetracked. If you truly desire something, and let your bee know, it will keep looking for solutions for you all the time, even when it looks like there is a roadblock in front of you.

It is also important so that you do not get stuck on one possibility. If you get stuck on one possibility and something happens where you cannot obtain it, what are you going to do? Instead of getting mad or depressed, you can just shift over to another solution to your intentions.

For example, if you have decided that the solution of having a baby is the best solution to your intention to feel and express love towards another, but you find out you can't get pregnant, what do you do? You can look at your other solutions that you came up with and pursue one of them. You could adopt a child, adopt a pet, join Big Brothers/Big Sisters, volunteer at a nursing home or hospital, take care of a community garden, cook a special dinner for your significant other, walk the neighbors dog, shovel the neighbor's sidewalk, or become a foster parent – the possibilities are endless. If you stay open to the options, you will find another way to fulfill your desire.

So always stay in the process and keep the bee on the job!

"Obstacles are things a person sees when he takes his eyes off his goal."
– E. Joseph Cossman

Takeaway: Always stay open to possibilities, even after you have started pursuing a possible solution.

Unscribbling Exercise 6 –

Review your worksheets that list your intentions. Then flip them all into a question. "How can I ___?" On separate pieces of paper, put your question in the middle of each page, then do a little brainstorming just to get some ideas out of your head. Keep the paper handy and as your bee sends back possible solutions, write them down. Keep doing this until you find a possible solution that feels right and that you want to try to explore.

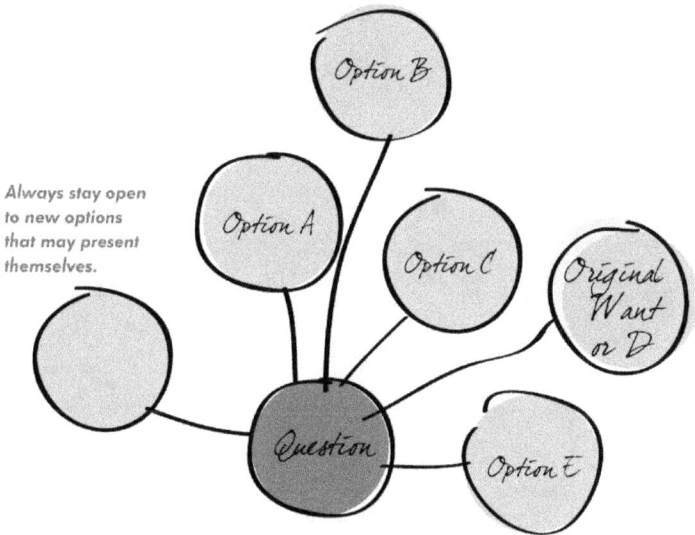

Always stay open to new options that may present themselves.

Option B

Option A

Option C

Original Want or D

Question

Option E

For Example…

An option...
Build up a savings account

An option...
Create a balanced budget for myself and stick to it

An option...
Start and contribute to a retirement savings account

An option...
NEED less money to sustain my life

An option...
Make sure I have enough insurance

An option...
Get a sugar mamma or daddy

Question...
How can I feel financially secure?

An option...
Get rid of my debt

An option...
Create a stream of residual income

An option...
Get more clients so if one goes away I am not vulnerable

An option...
Invest in a secure investment

An option...
Invest in a house

Note how the original "want" has become just one solution of many that might fulfill your true desire.

IMPORTANT: Always leave room for more option that your bee is yet to discover!

EXTRAS
Download a copy of this worksheet at:
http://www.unscribbling.com/extras

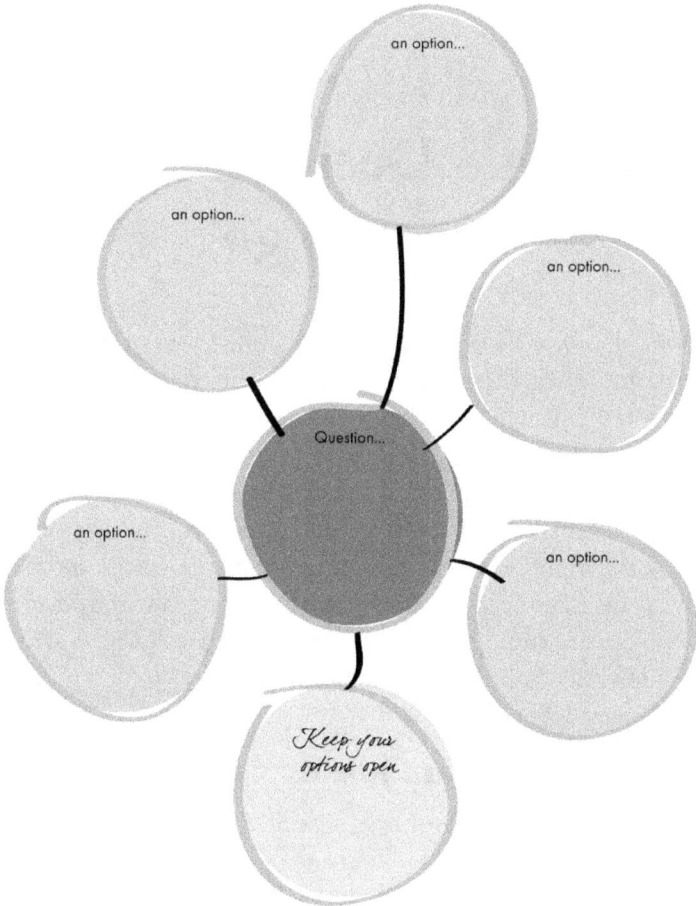

an option...

an option...

an option...

Question...

an option...

an option...

Keep your
options open

Step 4 – Deciding which way to go

Now that you have looked for possibilities, it's time to explore one (or more) of them. But which one do you explore? No one else can tell you which is the best solution for you. This is a task that only the people involved in the situation can truly decide. Get other people's opinions if that helps, but ultimately you need to make the final decision. But the question is: how do you know what is the right solution to pursue? This can be a moment of paralysis for many people. Decisions are scary! But they don't have to be. Here are some points to keep in mind when you are trying to decide which solution to pursue:

You are just exploring

No matter which solution you decide to pursue, keep in mind that the decision is not set in stone. Even if it were, you could always break the stone if you wanted. By keeping your eye on your INTENTION, not your chosen SOLUTION, it does not really matter which solution you choose right now.

Sometimes, as you pursue a solution, you learn that it might not be the right one after all. Forcing yourself to continue down that path is forcing yourself towards a solution that no longer works. What sense is there in that? You can make your decision, explore that solution, gather new information, and guess what? You can change your mind if you want to.

Instead of thinking of your decision as "charting a course for the rest of your life," think of this decision as "what do I want to explore right now?"

All you are choosing is what to EXPLORE. And how fun is it to explore? Remember, it is okay to change your mind at any time.

> *"When you force solutions to problems,*
> *you only create more problems."*
> *- Deepak Chopra*

Takeaway: Whatever solution you decide to explore, know that you are just exploring. You are free to change your mind and explore another solution if the one you choose no longer works.

Your feelings might be showing you the way

As we discussed before, your emotions can be an internal guidance system. Ask yourself:
- Which of these solutions gets me the most excited?
- Which solution do my eyes keep going back to?
- If I had all the money in the world, which one would I go for?
- What feels the best or the most fun?

Look for the solution that is resonating with you and then move on to the next step.

> *"Always follow your gut instinct about what to do, even if it is*
> *different from what I've told you. If you don't and the you fail, you*
> *won't take responsibility for the failure, which means it won't provide*
> *you with the lesson you need to learn."*
> *- Norm Brodsky, Inc. Magazine July/August 2009*

Takeaway: Your feelings can guide you to the best solution. Follow where they lead.

Is it a win–win–win?

Another gauge you can use is to ask yourself if the solution is a win–win–win. Do all people involved with this solution win? This is especially important in business and family transactions. As Napoleon Hill says, "Engage in no transaction which does not benefit all whom it affects." Ask yourself:
- Is this the best solution for me and the business (or family)?
- Is it best for our customers?
- What about our employees?
- Is it the best for the community and the environment?

Whomever your solution may touch, make sure they are considered. For instance, if your possible solution affects the whole community, ask, "Is this the best decision for the next seven generations?" Seven!? That's right, seven! This "think seven generations ahead" philosophy was one that we had to keep in mind when designing the Art Center. It is one of the Oneida Nation's fundamental beliefs. Can you imagine what good decisions we would make if everyone considered the ramification of our choices on the next seven generations? For instance, do you put up condos all over town willy–nilly, or do you plan some park space, bike trails and places for agriculture?

When you've hit upon a solution that is best for all involved, you are probably going down a good path. If it feels right, explore it!

"My basic principle is that you don't make decisions because they are easy; you don't make them because they are cheap; you don't make them because they're popular; you make them because they're right."
– Theodore Hesburgh

Takeaway: Engage in no transaction which does not benefit all whom it affects.

Additional techniques to explore:

1. Imagine the future with your choice

If you are still having a hard time deciding, try Victor E. Frankl's approach from Man's Search for Meaning and "Live as if you were living already for the second time and as if you had acted the first time as wrongly as you are about to act now!" It's a confusing sentence, but basically, it is saying to look at the choices in front of you. Imagine picking one. Now imagine yourself 10 or 20 years in the future. What do you think of your future self? Is your future self happy? If your future self could do it all over again, would she? Examine the choice that you made and where it has brought your future self. Is this what you want? If yes, then your present self knows how to proceed. If no, then your present self knows to look at other options.

2. Muscle Testing or Applied Kinesology

Muscle testing is a body feedback technique where you measure the response of your muscles to determine if the thought (or vibrations) of something empowers your body or makes you feel weak. When I tried it, I was impressed at the accuracy. Basically, your body gets stronger if something is right, and weaker if something is wrong or bad for you. If you have a partner who can help, try sticking your arm out straight at your side. Say, "My name is____." Use your real name. Then have your partner try to moderately push down on your arm. It probably won't move much. Now say something false, and your arm will be pushed down easily. Now apply this to bigger questions, like "would it be good for me to _____" and see what your body tells you. If you don't have a partner who can help, loop your fingers so your pointer finger and your thumb form a circle, like an okay sign. Stick the forefinger of your other hand inside the circle. Ask your question, then try to swipe your finger between where your pointer finger and thumb meet. "Yes" answers should be harder to break through, and "no" answers should slide through more easily.

Cool, huh? To learn more about muscle testing, you can explore the book *Power vs Force* by Dr. David R. Hawkins.

SSN – Picking a direction
http://bit.ly/SSN-Picking

> *"Certain things catch our eye. But pursue only those things that capture your heart."*
> *– Native American Saying*

Step 5 – Exploring; transforming the dream(er) to a vision(ary)

So you have identified your desires, set your intention, brainstormed and found a solution that feels right to you (even though you are staying open to other options). Now the work begins! It's time to put up or shut up!

Perhaps I am not the most patient friend a person could have. If someone is going on and on about a dream or a problem and is doing NOTHING about it – it drives me insane! (I have actually "broken up" with a few friends over things like this.)

Don't get me wrong, if a friend is telling me about a desire or a problem they are having, I am 100 percent ready to help them figure it out and move forward. But when someone tells me about the same problem for the 20th time, and they have done nothing about it... well, then I am probably only 15 percent on board. In order to fix problems or fulfill your desires, you have to take action at some point. You are going to need to start to explore one of your options. If all you are doing is talking about it, do me (and all your friends and family) a favor, and shut up! I, and probably everyone else you have been telling this to, are sick of hearing the broken record.

We want to help you, but you need to be willing to do some work. So let's look at how you can make your intentions come to fruition.

Dreams to visions

So you have gone through the process of imagining the possibilities, and you have found a solution that you want to explore. That possible solution now becomes a dream – or an aspiration, goal or aim. You are now the dreamer – a person who dreams. Being a dreamer is a fun place to be. It's all possibilities and hope, but it is just a starting point. Now you need to become a visionary – let me steal a quote here:

> "The difference between a dreamer and a visionary is that the visionary takes steps to make the dream happen."
> – Ron Fox

Where the dreamer imagines a result, a visionary sees the path to get there and follows.

So how do you find your path? Reverse-bubble it!

Take the solution you have decided to explore, and start asking yourself, "What do I have to do to make this happen?" Once you list all of the actions you can think of, ask yourself that same question about all of the things you listed. Keep going in reverse from your solution until you get to an action you can easily take now to go forward.

For instance, if the solution is "Get more clients," ask, "What do I have to do to make this happen?"

Possible answers:
- Get the word out about my business.
- Ask existing clients and friends for referrals.
- Sign up and check out websites that post freelance positions and gigs.
- _____ (Keep your options open!)

Do you see how this process mirrors the brainstorming of solutions? And that you are coming up with MULTIPLE options to achieve your solution? And that you are keeping your options open? Funny how that works, huh?

Now, from your new list, ask, "How do I get the word out about my business?" You could:
- Advertise.
- Go to networking events.
- Create a website and marketing material.
- Hire a salesperson.
- Make cold calls.
- _____ (Keep your options open!)

Now do it again. Let's look at, "Advertise." How do you advertise?
- Identify your target market.
- Create a marketing message.
- Create a media strategy.
- Create a brand/logo/identity.
- _____ (Keep your options open!)

Keep going until you get to steps that you can act on now. These reverse-bubbles become your path. This becomes your "To Do" list. Do NOT feel like you have to have everything in the right order or have all the possibilities for each completely thought out. You are just looking for your starting point. As you progress, you may discover new paths to add to your reverse bubble, or you may find solutions that let you shoot ahead (like the game Shoots and Ladders). That is why you:
1. Keep our options open at EVERY step of the way
2. Keep our eyes on the ultimate intention.

The reverse-bubble then becomes your tentative plan and working "to do" list.

"The secret of getting ahead is getting started. The secret of getting started is breaking your complex overwhelming tasks into small manageable tasks, and then starting on the first one."
- Mark Twain

Takeaway: Create your "To Do" list by stepping each option back with the questions, "What do I have to do to make this happen?"

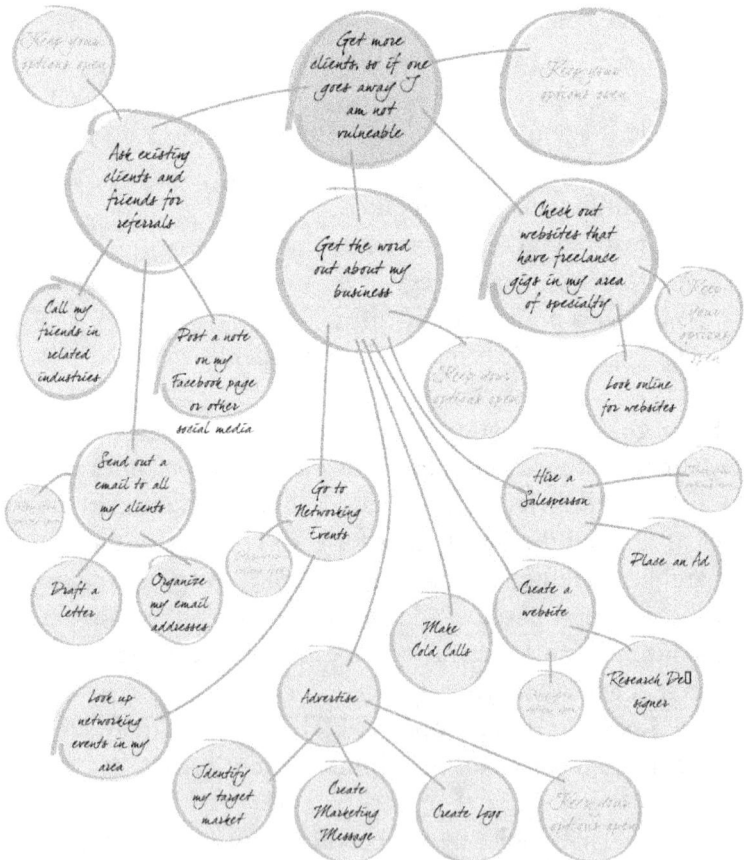

The importance of breaking it down into steps

Big, abstract concepts like "get more clients" can feel over-whelming. Where do you start? What do you do? When you start to feel overwhelmed, many people have a tendency to stick their heads in the sand and wait for the feeling to go away. But when you break down the stages of progression into doable parts, you can see the path and how to progress. It makes each step much less scary.

Of course, sometimes seeing all the parts can be just as scary! Just remember, you don't have to do it all at once. Focus on accomplishing the task at the start of the path. Work on that step and once it's complete you should be ready to take on the next step. Each step will prepare you for the next.

Doctors don't start out performing surgery on their first day. They study, then observe, then practice and eventually they are prepared to operate. Actors don't just go on stage and perform Shakespeare. They first read the play, analyze it, memorize their lines, rehearse with the other actors and then they perform it. In order for basketball players to become champions, they have to take it one game at a time. When you want to eat a meal, you don't shove the whole hamburger in your mouth, you take one bite at a time. But eventually you will have the whole thing eaten.

Breaking things into bite-sized bits and taking one step at a time will eventually get you where you want to be.

> *"First you write down your goal; your second job is to break down your goal into a series of steps, beginning with steps which are absurdly easy."*
> *– Fitzhugh Dodson*

Takeaway: By breaking down the path into steps, and taking one step at a time, you will eventually get where you want to be.

Now start doing the things on the list!

Did you decide that you want to start with the networking

path? Okay. Look up networking events in your area. Now you found some events that look interesting and are just waiting for the events... well, don't just sit around! What is another path you can start going down at the same time? Have you gotten as far as you can go with that path for now? Go down another path. Now it's time for a networking event? Perfect. Go down that path again.

The point is:

1. Do something. Take a step.
2. There is always a path or a step that you can take and explore.

But it all starts with that first step. My friend, Keith, posted on his Facebook page, "one hour down... approximately 1999 to go..." I had to inquire. Turns out, he is working towards his helicopter pilot's license. He had just done his first hour of training, but needs 2000 hours to get his license. He's not there yet, but he is on his way. He only has 1999 to go!

What first step do you need to take to fulfill your desires? Take the step.

> *"The journey of a thousand miles begins with one step."*
> *– Lao Tzu*

Takeaway: Start doing the things on your list.

Moments of pause are not failure

Kind of tired out from pursuing clients? Okay, take a break. Just because you need a break does not mean that you stop and never return to the path. When and if the inspiration hits you to return to a path – do it. But don't write off the path completely because you are temporarily tired or have other priorities.

My friend, Sharon, is an aspiring writer. She is very talented and has an interesting story to tell. But as life got hectic and the writing reached a difficult point, she contemplated quitting. But why? There is no deadline. She can set aside the writing for years, and pick it up again later. Stopping completely would be a shame. Telling herself, "I'm done. I can't do this," will make it harder to return if she ever feels inclined.

Pauses are common for my clients when we develop their websites. They often come back to me and apologize for the delay. I always tell them, "Websites have a timeline of their own. It will come to life when it comes to life. As long as we don't have a deadline we HAVE to hit, it's all okay." It is always refreshing to see them relax after this. (Plus, they are the client, they can delay things all they want. Who am I to say anything differently?)

Taking a break or shifting your focus is natural, and for most people, inevitable at times. Family illnesses, job transfers, deaths, a crying baby, the dog needs to pee, you have no clean clothes to wear, anything could signal that your priorities need to shift for awhile. Whether that shift lasts years or minutes, the break is natural and needed. Whatever might be distracting you is there. You can't ignore it. Deal with it and come back to your path when you are ready. But don't beat yourself up or tell yourself you can never pursue your path again. Keep your options open.

> *"A black cat crossing your path signifies*
> *that the animal is going somewhere."*
> *– Groucho Marx*

I want to clarify this quote. Basically, don't read so much into a delay or make it more important than it really is. It's there, but it doesn't mean that you should turn around and run home.

Takeaway: If you need to take a break from the path for a while, take a break. If you like the path there is no sense in giving up completely.

You can take more than one path at a time

As I said, distractions are natural. For me, a path that has often been abandoned has been this book. When I have had time to work on it, I do. But when I have had client projects to work on, I work on those instead. (After all, I have to pay the bills.) I always came back to working on the book eventually. Sometimes it has taken months, but I always came back. Since you are reading it you know I finished it eventually. I also have another book that has been on the shelf for about thirteen years. Maybe someday I will return to it. But I am not giving up on any of my projects. When I pick them up again, I always enjoy them. I just need to be patient with myself and remember that a break from them does not mean that they are dead, that I have failed or that I can never return to them.

One of my favorite lines from a movie is from Under the Tuscan Sun. One of the characters gives advice to Diane Lane's character from the late Federico Fellini, which is, "You have to live spherically, in many directions, and never loose your childish enthusiasm and then things will come your way."

Live spherically, my friends, with childish enthusiasm! With enough determination, time and patience you will eventually fulfill the desire at the end of your path. And if you are taking more than one path at a time, enjoy whatever project your whims put you on that day.

> *"The whole secret of life is to be interested in one thing profoundly and in a thousand things well."*
> *— Horace Walpole*

Takeaway: Live spherically and pursue as many paths as you can.

Be open to changing gears?

After exploring a path for a while you may actually decide that, in fact, this is not the right path for you. Okay, no problem, try something else. Remember you are just exploring! Investigate and explore the path that you think is best for you until it no longer feels right. IF that happens, look at your solutions again and see if there is a better path for you to explore. You will have learned something, so take that new knowledge with you down your new path.

Jane, an acquaintance of mine, went to school to become a teacher. When it was time for her to do student teaching, she went to the school, tried it for week and decided she hated being in the classroom and never wanted teach again. So she shifted gears and tried something else. I like to think she will be happier in the long run, and I hope she was able to find what was behind her wanting to be a teacher fulfilled another way. Perhaps she really desired "to educate the future" and is now a textbook writer!

Either way, this was not a situation where she just needed a break from the path. She knew without a doubt that she was on the wrong path. So she did something about it. For that I admire her.

"It's never too late to change the direction of your life. If you were driving in your car and realized you were headed in the wrong direction, you would turn around; why not do that with your life?"
– Ron Fox

Takeaway: If a path no longer feels right, explore another path.

Stay open to other options!

I know I am beating a dead horse here, but I cannot over-emphasize the importance of staying open to whatever your little bee might find. You never know what new ideas might come up as you travel down your path.

"When you know how, you are thinking too small – way more is possible. Stay open to the possibilities. Look at everything you have in life – nothing came into your life the way you thought it would come. Trust the universe. If you have to come up with some 'How tos' to do that do, but don't become attached!"
– Matthew Ferry

Do something!

Now it is time for you to take action. For the love of Pete, don't make me write you off too. Take a step. Do something! Transform yourself from a dreamer to a visionary! It all starts with the first step.

"Success is never wondering what if."
- Karrie Huffman

"When you believe you can do it, the how–to–do–it develops."
– Eric Butterworth

And, one of my favorite quotes ever...

"When you pray, move your feet."
–Quakers

SSN - Yes, you need to take action!
http://bit.ly/SSN-Action

Exercise 7 – Reverse-Bubble

Take your chosen solution and reverse-bubble it back to a point where you can start to take action on the paths. Then take action!

Step 6 – Thank

Once your desires have been fulfilled, don't forget to thank anyone and everyone who helped you fulfill your desires. I know this may seem obvious, but for some people it's not. So say, "thank you." Express your gratitude to everyone who played a part. For the more you thank, the more you will find to be thankful for.

Replay the "Thank you" game from the brainstorming section. Finish by saying, "Thank you for all of the wonderful ways my desires were fulfilled. What else can I do to increase this feeling of gratefulness?"

And to steal a line I learned from Rikka Zimmerman, ask "How does life get better than this?" What a way to show gratitude and tell your bee to go off and find new ways to make life even better.

> *"Sometimes our light goes out but is blown into flame by another human being. Each of us owes deepest thanks to those who have rekindled this light."*
> *–Albert Schweitzer*

Takeaway: Remember to thank anyone who has helped you to fulfill your desires.

SSN The Momentum of Thanking
http://bit.ly/SSN-Thanking

Part 2

Things to keep in mind while unscribbling

You are worthy of your desires

You can wish all you want for a better job, a perfect relationship, more money, or whatever your want or desires may be, but if you don't think you deserve to have your desires fulfilled – if you don't KNOW you deserve it – you probably won't realize your dreams no matter how hard you try. You will talk yourself out of getting it. Or you will get whatever you want and sabotage the situation and lose it.

Why? Because people naturally gravitate toward where they feel comfortable. If you don't feel worthy of your dreams and desires, it will be extremely hard for you to live in a state where your desires are met. Your subconscious will work to bring you back to a "comfortable" state, so living with your desires fulfilled will not be possible.

"We do not believe in ourselves until someone reveals that deep inside us something is valuable, worth listening to, worthy of our trust, sacred to our touch. Once we believe in ourselves we can risk curiosity, wonder, spontaneous delight or any experience that reveals the human spirit."
– e. e. cummings

Takeaway: You must believe you are worthy of having your desires met in order to achieve and hold on to them.

We are ALL deserving

The good news is that we are all worthy and deserving of having our deepest desires met. WE ARE!!! And I can prove it...

Don't worry, I'm not going to give you a spiritual speech about equality. I believe in it, but I am not going to give you that speech. As I mentioned before, we'll keep the spiritual stuff out of the book. Instead I have two key points to make:

1. When it rains, it rains on all just the same – sinner and saint. Both the weed and the orchid have equal opportunity to grow, and usually do.

Okay, that was a little spiritual, but I think you get my point. We are all equal; therefore, if one is worthy, we all are.

But, it's not so much a matter of proving that we are all worthy, it's about YOU FEELING worthy. So how can you start to feel worthy?

This brings me to point #2:

2. Whatever happened in the past to make you feel unworthy, doesn't matter. It's the past! In this new moment, I really don't give a rats patootie what horrible thing you think you've done in your past; how you did not apply yourself in school, how you hurt someone, how people told you that you were no good, or even how you may have had an impure thought or two.

It truly does not matter what your past actions, inactions or thoughts have been. Each life begins anew with each new second. With each new second you are capable of changing your direction. You are capable of choosing thoughts and actions that make you feel worthy. Therefore, you are worthy, because you have the choice to be worthy.

Feeling worthy is a choice and choice is something that, thankfully, we are all awarded in life. It's called free will, baby!

Feeling worthy comes from doing, saying, and being a person you feel is worthy. What makes you feel worthy will probably be different than what makes your friend feel worthy. It will be different for each individual, so remember to "be who you is" and do things that make YOU feel worthy, and don't worry about what others think.

Just as you can transform any situation, problem, action, inaction or thought into a turning point that is moving you closer to fulfilling your deepest desires, you can stop having negative thoughts about yourself. You can see yourself as worthy. It simply comes down to a choice.

Say to yourself,

> "Today I see myself as worthy, because today I choose to be worthy, act worthy, say and do worthy things. I am deserving of having all of my deepest dreams and desires come true, because I am worthy."

And even if you slip a little, each second starts a new opportunity. So if you feel yourself slipping into unworthiness, stop, rethink and start anew with actions and thoughts that make you feel worthy. If you go forward empowered with the knowledge that you can change your direction, ready and able to tackle anything, and knowing you are worthy and deserve good things, you can obtain anything you desire. If you go forward feeling unworthy, what do you think is going to happen? The choice is yours.

"Worthiness, or unworthiness, is something that is pronounced upon you by you. You are the only one that can deem yourself worthy or unworthy. You are the only one who can love yourself into a state of allowing, or hate yourself in a state of disallowing."
– Abraham (Jerry and Ester Hicks)

Takeaway: You are worthy. Feeling worthy is a choice. You have the power to feel worthy.

Is it really that simple?

Could life really be that simple? Can you just start thinking of yourself as worthy and the world will fall into place for you? That might depend a little on what you have done in your past. Just because we are worthy does not mean we are instantly entitled to the support of our loved ones, or anyone else for that matter. It does depend on what you put out there.

People think of karma as our past lives or actions affecting our present. And they CAN... well, I am not 100 percent sure about the past lives, but your past ACTIONS can definitely affect your present.

For instance, if you have been a jerk in the past, getting other people to support you in realizing your dreams and desires is probably going to be harder than if you have been a big sweetie. But the point is you can transform how you interact with others NOW, creating a new karma for yourself going forward.

My friend, Sean, has been back and forth in a battle against alcohol for as long as I can remember. His "slips" have caused him to lose jobs, girlfriends, friends and the end of his finger. Each time he has decided to get cleaned up, he has to go forward, often without the support of people who once loved and cared about him, or with their skepticism. He has to live with that karma, but it does not make him unworthy of love and being cared about. BUT, each moment he decides to stay clean, meet his responsibilities and treat his loved ones with respect, he creates a new karma for himself. In each new moment he gets to decide what kind of karma he will create for himself going forward. He might be creating it with new people, but he is still in control of making good or bad choices to create his karma.

Your past is your past. You cannot go back and change that. But you can change how you act now, and act in ways that make you feel worthy of support going forward.

"Destiny is not a matter of chance, it is a matter of choice."
- W.J. Bryan

"This does not mean our past wrong thoughts need bother us forever. We can neutralize them by deliberate choice of the good."
– Dr. Fredrick Bailes

Takeaway: Whatever is in your past is done but you can change your future with your actions in the present. By changing your actions now, you will start to feel worthy.

Stop doing whatever makes you feel unworthy

If you are not feeling worthy, you need to change something. I know change is a big scary word, but if you stay as you are, don't you think you are going to get more of the same? Accept yourself for who you are, but don't be afraid to change yourself.

I once had a boyfriend who told me "I'm sorry" about ten times a day for various things. The words stopped meaning anything. He was not sorry. He went ahead and did whatever he was going to do, thinking the words "I'm sorry" would make up for any transgressions. I finally said, "Just stop doing things that you have to apologize for!"

What a revelation – Stop doing things that make you feel like you are unworthy!

If you think, "I'll never be good enough for that promotion, because I can't seem to get to work on time." ... Ah, drrr, set your alarm clock earlier. Or better yet, let's UNSCRIBBLE the desire here...

Step 1– Become aware of your desire

I WANT a promotion. Because I DESIRE...
  – more money
  – the confidence that comes from being a manager
  – people to respect me
  – to learn new things
  – to challenge myself
  – to be the "boss"

Okay, I've thought about it, and when it comes down to it, I really desire more money.

Sidenote: I'm going to use the example of money here, as many people feel this way. But money is NOT a true desire. It is NOT an experience or a feeling, but since it works to show you how to kick yourself in the ass and make a few changes in your life, I'm going to use it for now. (See Part 2, Chapter 2 – "You don't really desire money" for more on how money is NOT a desire.)

Step 2– Intend

"I intend to have more money."

Step 3 – Question and Brainstorm

What ways can I have more money?
  – Get a promotion.
  – Get a second job.
  – Spend less money.
  – Sell some of my things.
  – Get rid of cable TV.
  – Get a job with a different company that pays better.
  – Ask my employer for a raise.
  – See if my employer has any additional work I could do on a contract basis on my own time.
  – _____ (Remember to leave yourself open to new solutions)

Step 4 & 5 – Deciding and exploring

Okay, right now in this moment, a promotion is the solution that is most appealing to me. I am open to other opportunities, but what do I need to do to achieve that?

– Show I am responsible.
– Demonstrate that I am dedicated.
– Let my employer know that I want a promotion (they might not know).
– Perform my job to the best of my abilities and keep learning how to perform even better.
– Ask to learn new skills that I would need in the promoted position.
– _____ (Keep myself open to fun unexpected ways to show I am ready for a promotion.)

So how do I:

– Show I am responsible?
– Get to work on time.
– Work when I am at work. (instead of checking my fantasy football stats or what's happening on Facebook)
– Get my work done on time or ahead of time.
– Mentor another person in my office.

Keep following the process. Reverse-bubble each of the above to get to actionable steps you can take now.

So how do you "get to work on time?" You could set your alarm earlier and get your butt to work on time!

So there is an actionable step. But, now you are coming up with excuses, aren't you? "Oh, but once I am up playing video games I just can't stop."

Yeah, you can! Put the console down or don't pick it up. What-ever you think you can't stop doing that is prohibiting you from realizing your desires – STOP DOING IT!

It's a matter of long–term happiness versus instant gratification. Which is ultimately going to be better for you? The happiness that will come from going to bed at a reasonable time, getting to work on time and getting that promotion? Or the instant gratification of getting the high score on Donkey Kong?

Still think you just can't stop? Think of it this way. You are a teenager. Your parents are out for the evening. You are making out on your parent's couch, and your horny teenage boyfriend whines, "but I can't stop." Then you see the flash of headlights on the wall as your parents car pulls into the driveway.

What happens? He stops. You both scramble, and rearrange your disheveled clothes to make yourself presentable. But he stopped. He COULD stop. And so can you! (Can you imagine the scene if he really could not? Ridiculous, isn't it?)

So if you are telling yourself that you "can't stop" doing something that is holding you back, think of yourself as a randy teenage boy who just saw the headlights – and stop. If Randy can stop with all those hormones running through his body, you can stop whatever it is you are doing. Use this current second as the second you remember that you are worthy and change your actions.

If it is negative thoughts that are holding you back, put a rubber band on your wrist. Every time you start to think negatively, flick your wrist with it. It really does help you stop the thoughts. When I do this, after I flick the rubber band, I remind myself of a positive thought I have already memorized to replace the negative thought.

If you need help beating negative thoughts, ask a friend to help you. Ask them to fine you every time they hear you say something negative about yourself. (This can work with any behavior you are trying to modify.)

Drop your excuses. Act and think in ways that make you feel worthy, and know you are worthy.

"Your problem is you are too busy holding on to your unworthiness."
- Ram Dass

Takeaway: Start believing that you are worthy. Stop actions, in–actions and thinking in ways that make you feel unworthy.

For a bit of fun… Watch the Video by Mad TV called "Stop It!"
http://bit.ly/Extra-StopIt

SSN– Clearing your mind of negative thoughts
http://bit.ly/SSN-Clearing

P.S. For other thoughts on ways to change behavior, I highly recommend the book Switch by Chip and Dan Heath. Go to http://www.heathbrothers.com/switch/ for more information.

Is the role you play making you feel unworthy?

Sometimes you can get stuck in roles and have a hard time breaking out of them. Whatever role you played in your family dynamic, or whatever stereotype you fit in does not matter. You don't have to play that role forever. You can choose to define your "character" however you want.

Were you told you were not good enough? So you go around never getting things done. Was your sister the pretty one? So you hide your beauty, because you are the brainy one and you'll never be as pretty as your sister anyway. Were you the funny one in the family and not the smart one, so no one expects you to do anything substantial in your life? So, as long as you are making people laugh nobody cares that you can't hold a job. Throw those roles out the window! Don't let a past role you have played define you! If you want to do something, DO IT! Even if it is out of character with how people have seen you before. Who knows, they might like the new you even better.

The same goes for stereotypes. Do you fit a stereotype and feel like you can't get past your environment and what people think of you? Screw that! You can rise above what you look like and what your environment is. Every person in a demographic who thinks that they are not capable of greatness is WRONG. I can guarantee that if you looked, you would find an example from your demographic who has risen to heights that the others have not even dreamt possible.

Do you live in a bad neighborhood? Ummm, hello! That's the stuff movies are made of. Get your butt in a seat at the library and study, even if you have to sneak through the roof to do it to avoid the gun shots.

Whatever excuse you come up with for what is holding you back, there is someone in a similar situation who was able to make their life happy, healthy, functioning and even thriving. Where there is a will there is a way. You do not need to play into the roles of family dynamics or be bound by the demographic or situation you were born into. EACH SECOND OF YOUR LIFE IS A CHOICE. You can choose to "play a role" or you can choose to feel worthy and be extraordinary.

You just need determination, to know you can succeed, to know you are worthy, and to find ways to do it. (Unscribble the problem.) We've all had to overcome our personal stereotypes in one form or another. Looking a certain way is no excuse for not achieving. (Try being blonde and having big boobs and be taken seriously for your intellect.) Yes, it may be harder for you, but there are successful people in every shape, color and what not. They have done it. SO CAN YOU.

"I don't think of myself as a poor, deprived ghetto girl who made good. I think of myself as somebody who from an early age knew I was responsible for myself, and I had to make good."
– Oprah Winfrey

Takeaway: It does not matter what demographic you fit, or what role you played in your past. In this present second, you can choose to live your life differently.

Are you holding yourself back so others don't feel uncomfortable?

Do you know you are qualified and worthy, but you are holding yourself back so that others aren't uncomfortable? STOP IT! What good is that going to do? (See sidenote "So, who are you?" in Part 1, Step 1, in the section titled "'Rules' to keep in mind about identifying your desires")

In college I took a leadership position in a class group project. I kept trying to back away from the leadership position trying to give someone else a chance to step up and take the lead. I thought it would be better if everyone had a chance to experience the leadership role. But no one would step up. I was discussing this issue with Adrian, a student in the class above me who also seemed to find himself in the leadership position. I asked him how I could get someone else to be the leader. He gave me some great advice. He looked me straight in the eye and said, "Fuck 'em! If they don't step up on their own, that's their problem. You step up and be great!" I thought, "Holy crap! Can you do that?" Wow! Those words changed my life. (Thank you, Adrian.)

Women especially need to learn not to hold themselves back in order to give someone else a chance or avoid overshadowing their mates. Everyone's greatness has to come from within themselves! You can lead by example. If they ask you for help and you are in a position to help them, of course, help them. But ONLY if they ask. Until they want it themselves, "fuck 'em!" Remember, you cannot change them for "their own good," and you will not help people grow by holding yourself back. Others need to want to change and grow on their own.

You keep changing, growing and reaching for your desires. That is the only way we can make the world a better place. It starts from our individual actions. The only person you can change is yourself. Know you are capable of change and so is everyone else. But they won't change until they desire to. All you can do is show them the way with your example, and help them if they ask. And always, always shine YOUR light as an example.

> *"Our deepest fear is not that we are inadequate. Our deepest fear is that we are powerful beyond measure. It is our light, not our darkness, that frightens us most. We ask ourselves, 'Who am I to be brilliant, gorgeous, talented, and famous?' Actually, who are you not to be? You are a child of God. Your playing small does not serve the world. There is nothing enlightened about shrinking so that people won't feel insecure around you. We were born to make manifest the glory of God that is within us. It's not just in some of us; it's in all of us. And when we let our own light shine, we unconsciously give other people permission to do the same. As we are liberated from our own fear, our presence automatically liberates others."*
> (Used by Nelson Mandela in his 1994 inaugural speech)
> – Maryanne Williamson

Takeaway: Let your light shine. Inspire others to greatness by example, NOT by holding yourself back.

Stop using external validation to determine your worthiness

You are worthy of great things. Even if you don't have the best education, or you don't have much money in the bank, or you are single, etc. etc. etc. When your identity is attached to external validations, like the love of another, a high paying job, your kid's success, your peer's approval of you, how big your house is or how nice your car is, you are putting yourself in a very vulnerable position. You will feel great as long as all of those things are meeting your expectations, but what happens if or when they don't?

What happens if your kid does something horrible at school? Or you suddenly lose your job? Or you get into a car accident? Or the person you are dating ends things? Or the stock market takes a plunge taking your money with it? Or the value of your house drops?

If you are using those external things to gauge your worthiness, you're placing your value in someone else's hands. Know you are worthy and maintain your confidence from the inside.

So she dumped you; does that mean you are less of a man? So your job went away; did you stop being as skilled and talented as you were when you had the job? YOU are YOU with or without the external things so don't let them determine your worthiness.

A great moment came in my life when I realized I no longer had to prove to others that I was intelligent (and therefore worthy of their acceptance). I attended a dinner party for a friend who has a wicked sense of humor and is always joking around. So I was ready for a ton of laughs. There were four of us out at a nice restaurant in Chicago. Instead of a bunch of laughs, we were having a series of what I like to call "stupid yuppie conversations," where everyone tries to out-smart and out-cool each other by showing how much you know and who you know and how cool you are. Perhaps it was because I've tried to play that game before and failed, or I wanted to really enjoy my friend and have some laughs, or maybe it was because I had a couple of glasses of wine, but having a super serious discussion about whether Oprah's book club has had negative or positive impacts on the book world just seemed ridiculous. Who cared? Let's have some fun!

But I ended up loving that moment. It was the moment I realized that I didn't need to prove my intelligence and worthiness to the others. I knew I are intelligent, even if it doesn't always show. And even if they thought I was an idiot, who cared? I knew who I was. Their approval or disapproval did not effect what I knew of myself. I could look the fool and still know I was worthy.

It might not be a confidence that I'm able to carry off in all of my interactions, but in that moment I felt it. And I liked it – the moment I stopped relying on that external validation to judge my worthiness.

"We cannot choose our external circumstances, but we can always choose how we respond to them."
— Epictetus

Takeaway: Using external validation to determine your worth dis–empower you. Empower yourself from the inside out, not the other way around.

SSN– Where is your mood/worth coming from?
http://bit.ly/SSN-ComingFrom

Bonus: When you are empowered, everyone wants you!

Feeling you are worthy makes you feel empowered. Being empowered makes you attractive. It makes you attractive physically, as well as attractive to opportunities. What a bonus!

Who are the sexiest people in the world? The confident ones. Who do you want to be in charge of revamping part of your business? The confident one laying out a plan, or the one who is slumping in the corner waiting for a chance to speak? There is a reason the sexy and smart (no, no scratch that from your brain. It's the...) confident ones get all the opportunities. They exude empowerment and worth!

Empowerment, and knowing you are worthy, infuses you with an aura of attractiveness. Go get your sexy on!

"Self—worth comes from one thing —
thinking that you are worthy."
— Wayne Dyer

Takeaway: Feel worthy and attract opportunities galore!

P.S. Read Tim Sander's book Today we are Rich to learn more about "Harnessing the power of Total Confidence"

P.P.S. One more note on feeling worthy – you can get there through gratitude too…

"According to Plato's law, as you feel grateful, you become
attractive, not only in your beauty and radiance, but in your
relationships with people. More important, you release a vital
energy that draws to you opportunities, employment, and a
secure flow of substance."
— Erik Butterworth, "Spiritual Economics"

You don't really desire money

Money is great! I love money. I love having, spending, giving and using money. I think it is a great resource for experiencing life. (It's sure a lot easier to use then bartering with chickens.) Whether you idealize it, think it evil or have thoughts that lie somewhere in between, money is a reality of our existence and plays a huge role in our lives.

With money you can pay your bills, start a business, buy that sweet car you've had your eye on, take a vacation, get a mani-pedi, go to a restaurant, buy a house, go to college, remodel your house, get braces, pay for your child's private schooling, pay down your mortgage, invest in the stock market, put a water well in a deprived country, donate to a cause, build a mass transit system, launch a human to Mars... the possibilities are endless. Money can have a tremendous influence on our lives.

Even the THOUGHT of money can be influential. It can send you into depression, cause knots in your stomach, make you sigh with relief or fly high as a kite. Money can be absolutely intoxicating or make people look intoxicating, but why? Money is paper, or metal or just numbers on a balance sheet. Rather, money serves as a resource that can be used to fulfill our desires. That is why it is so appealing. Money is easily transferred to another and becomes a way to fulfill some of our desires.

But money can be more than just a resource for fulfillment. Money can also hold the key to some of our hidden desires. Money is a clue in the unscribbling process. After all, it is not really the money you desire, but the feelings and experiences it can provide that make it so desirable. So let's use our want of money to drill down to our true desires.

Unscribble it: What desires are behind YOUR want of money?

Fill in the following: If I was rich, or even if I just had an extra $10,000 lying around, I would...

1. _____
2. _____
3. _____
4. _____
5. _____

Now ask yourself, "why?" Why would you do/buy these things? Keep asking "why" until you get to the experience or feeling that you really desire. Money represents something to you. By following your "money trail" of wants, you will find your true desires.

We all have different things that make us tick, different ways we value money, and different things that we desire from our money. What do you want from your money? What experiences do you want your money to help bring about? What do you truly desire FROM your money resource?

"Money is only a tool. It will take you wherever you wish, but it will not replace you as the driver."
– Ayn Rand

Takeaway: Behind your want for money is a hidden desire. Keep following your wants until you find the experience or feeling you desire.

Money is not the only answer to fulfilling your desires

Money does seem like the be–all-end–all answer at times to fulfill many of your desires, but is it? What other ways, aside from money, are there to reaching your desires?

Once you find your desire, set your intention and go back to Step 3 of the unscribbling process – question and brainstorm, and think of ways that don't involve spending money or that spend little of it in order to gain what you desire. Remember, money is but one resource to fulfill your desires; the possibilities are endless if you open yourself up to them.

For instance, one of the reasons I desire money is so I can fly home and spend time with my family and friends. So with my intention to "be an active participant in the lives of my family and friends," (even though many of them live half a country away) I could...

- move closer to them so it would just be a quick drive to see them
- drive instead of fly to see them
- get a part-time job at an airline so I could get free "jump seats"
- beg them to visit me more often
- get a computer with a webcam so we could live chat with one another, and I can "be there" on the laptop as they sit around the camp fire
- call them more
- find a job that pays me to travel (Did you know some people drive cars across the country and get paid for it?)
- make new friends where I am
- _____ (Keep your options open!)

Just imagine the possibilities – some of these cost a little money, some cost no money and some MAKE me money. What other ways are there, aside from spending money, for you to be able to fulfill your desires?

"What's right about America is that although we have a mess of problems, we have great capacity – intellect and resources – to do some thing about them."
– Henry Ford

Takeaway: More money is NOT the only way to fulfill your desires but it is a resource that aids you in fulfilling your desires.

Money is not security

When you see money as a source of security in life, you put yourself in a vulnerable position. You are relying on something outside of yourself to bring you peace of mind. But money can be lost just as fast as it is found. You have to learn not to use the RESOURCE of money to gauge your security and peace of mind.

It is your thoughts, attitude and ability to adjust that can bring you true security and peace of mind, not money. I think Eric Butterworth said it best:

> "We have been erroneously conditioned to believe that our lives are completely shaped by what happens around us and to us. But life is lived from within–out. It is not what happens 'out there,' but what we do or think about what happens."

(See "Stop using external validation to determine your worthiness" in Part 2, Chapter 1 "You are worthy of your desires")

At the heart of this book, I hope to empower you with the ability to unscribble and solve your problems. With that ability security and peace of mind will follow. THAT is a way to security. (Well, that and maybe faith in God/the universe, but this book is not about that.)

Oddly enough, I bought a condo in my quest to feel financially secure, but the second it was mine I actually felt less financially secure than I have ever felt in my life. Suddenly, most of my savings was gone. Oh, and did I mention that at the same time I also had a disagreement with a business partner, and got screwed out of that investment? AND my biggest client suddenly decided not to do the project every year that brought in the bulk of my billable hours! Holy schnickies! And now I have a m–o–r–t–g–a–g–e... and if I can't pay that, all my savings are GONE and I am homeless. And since I used most of my savings to buy the place, I can't tap into that to pay the bills now that my income has declined. WHHHAAAHHH! Money was making me feel VERY insecure... I needed a paradigm shift!

I could not predict that my client would cut my hours, nor that my partner and I would have a "break it" argument, but I did have the ability to look for other solutions to solve my problems and fulfill my desires.

I desired and intended to keep the condo. So how could I do that? Let's brainstorm it. I could:
- Get a roommate
- Look for more clients
- Get a part-time or full-time job
- Start some kind of income producer of my own. Maybe selling art or Avon, or become a dog walker, or baby–sitter, or...
- Go out to restaurants less often with my friends.
- Drop my gym membership and start jogging instead.
The possibilities could go on and on.

By focusing on the lack of money and income my THOUGHTS were making me feel insecure. But by changing my thoughts, and keeping in my mind that, "whatever happens I can handle it and find new solutions" I felt empowered instead. No matter what my income level is, I can fall back on other solutions so I am not stuck – EVER. I have the ability to problem solve, to imagine possibilities and to develop a path to accomplishing whatever I desire. I am secure no matter how my income may vary. But with all that, I don't forget to stay open to even BETTER solutions that I might not have been able to imagine myself. Like:

Instead of living in my condo, perhaps I could move to California with my then-boyfriend, share the bills, and rent out my new condo. That was a path I never imagined during those dark days. But look how well it turned out! That boyfriend is now my husband and we now have rental property, which (eventually) is going to MAKE me money. Who could have guessed it?

Yes, it sure is nice to know that money is there if you need it, but it is even better to know that you have the ability to unscribble any situation that life throws at you! That is true security.

"If money is your hope for independence you will never have it. The only real security that a man will have in this world is a reserve of knowledge, experience, and ability."
– Henry Ford

Takeaway: Money is not the source of security, but your ability to solve problems (aka unscribbling) can be. Money is just a resource.

SSN– Money is not security
http://bit.ly/SSN-Money

Playing it Safe

Sometimes it seems easier to not do anything at all than to actively strive for your dreams and desires. If you don't take action, don't make changes, or don't try anything new in your life, you are playing it "safe." This strategy is fine if you are living with your desires fulfilled. But, if you are not, you're going to have to move out of your comfortable "safe" place in order to make your dreams happen.

I say "safe" in quotes, because safe is a matter of perspective, and it can be an illusion. A person living with an abusive partner might feel "safe" because it is what she knows. If she left and tried to live life another way, the way forward would feel unfamiliar and it might feel unsafe. By staying in your known/"safe" place you avoid possibly getting hurt by trying something new with your life. You get to feel/stay "safe". (I'll drop the quotes from here on out.)

The desire to feel safe and secure is instinctive, but that unconscious desire for security may be sabotaging our conscious desires from being fulfilled. In order to honor your desire for safety, it is important to learn how to feel secure while exploring new things and striving towards your desires.

Keeping everything exactly as it is currently is not the only way for you to create a sense of security. Life is dynamic. It is unrealistic to think things will not change. Your circumstances will change at some point whether you like it or not, but your sense of security can stay intact, and you can thrive no matter what life brings you.

As I mentioned in the section on money, "Money [or sameness] is not the source of security, but your ability to solve problems (aka unscribbling) can be." If you can unscribble, you are safe; you can solve whatever problem is before you. Knowing you can handle whatever is thrown at you can create a feeling of security.

In order to fulfill your conscious desires, you are more than likely going to need to break out of your sameness and do/try/explore/experience something new in your life and make a change.

When you find yourself opting to stay in your safe zone of sameness, ask yourself:
- What are you keeping yourself safe from? What unknown future are you able to avoid by staying in your safe place?
- What paradigm in your imagined future does not fit with your unique self?
- What past hurt are you projecting onto this new unknown future?
- Are you really a "victim" of your circumstances?
- Are you intimidated by the bigness of your desires?
- Are you procrastinating?
- What is the worst that can happen? (See next chapter, "What's the worst that can happen?")

"Growth means change and change involves risk, stepping from the known to the unknown."
–George Shinn

Takeaway: Feeling safe and secure does not have to come from sameness. In order to succeed in your desires you will more than likely need to explore something new.

SSN Sameness is not security either...
http://bit.ly/SSN-Sameness

What are you keeping yourself safe from? What unknown future are you able to avoid by staying in your safe place?

When you fantasize about what your future will be like once your desires are fulfilled, there are often parts of your imagined life that make you uncomfortable or tap into your fears. In order to avoid the scary parts, you may sabotage your desire rather than deal with the imagined bogeymen that came along for the ride.

Think of an actor who wants to be famous, yet when she imagines what that will be like, she sees:

- A disconnect with her current friends because they would not be able to handle her success.
- Her privacy becoming non-existent – have you seen all those pictures of celebrity's butts as they sunbathe?
- No longer having time to cook or garden or do the little things she loves because movie stars have long hours, they can't do those things.

Even though the aspiring actor consciously desires to be successful, unconsciously she may be trying to avoid it as she see all these negative aspects coming along with the positive. In order to avoid all these negatives, she might be late for auditions, not get enough sleep the night before or forget her lines – creating circumstances where success is not possible. This keeps her safe from her imaged problems that might come along with her success.

If you are getting cut off at the pass before you reach your desires, I would guess that you are creating circumstances that are keeping you safe or in sameness, because you are scared. Keep in mind that whatever future you are imagining, is just in your imagination. It's not real and it is not how things have to be for you.

It's like when you were a kid, and you thought there was a bogeyman is in your closet. This is the same thing! By keeping the door closed you never have to face the big scary monster. (Metaphorically speaking, of course, odds are there is no monster.) But you also never get to wear the shirt you love that you know is in there. Or rediscover that great pair of shoes you forgot you had.

Or find the present that your parents hid in there. Your imagination creates bogeymen that exist in your unknown future, where treasures might also be found. You need to find ways to tame your bogeymen so that you can get to your treasures.

Whatever unsafe future you have imagined is ONLY in your imagination, and is ONLY a possibility of how things could be. You do not know for a fact that the future you are imagining will include the bogeymen you are dreaming up.

You do not know for a fact that if you land that job you won't be able to find affordable housing in the city where your new job is located. Perhaps there is a great little neighborhood about a mile away that you don't know about.

You do not know for a fact that if you suggest an idea at the meeting, people will think you are ridiculous. Perhaps that will be the brilliant idea that keeps everyone working and earns you a promotion.

You do not know for a fact that if you get a full-time job, you will not have time to be a good parent. Perhaps feeling more fulfilled will make your time with your child even better.

You do not know for a fact that if you go back to school you will go into debt and be paying for it the rest of your life. Perhaps the new job that you will be qualified for after you get your degree will come with a signing bonus and you can pay off your school loans faster than you imagined.

Whatever bogeymen you have imagined exists only in your imagination. You do NOT know for a fact what your life will be like. The bogeymen probably don't exist or will not be as scary or bad as you imagine them to be. If they are real, just unscribble a way to deal with it. No big deal.

"Security is mostly a superstition. It does not exist in nature, nor do the children of men as a whole experience it. Avoiding danger is no safer in the long run than outright exposure. Life is either a daring adventure, or nothing."
– Helen Keller

Takeaways: Whatever you image your future to look like is not necessarily what the reality will be.

If you are self-sabotaging, you are keeping yourself safe and letting the bogeymen win.

Do you have a paradigm in your imagined future that does not fit with your unique self?

Your life is meant to be expressed in a manner fitting your unique self. Oftentimes your bogeymen are just preconceived notions about how you think something is SUPPOSED to look and function. Although the paradigms you have about life CAN serve as models they do not HAVE to be the way you live your life.

In an oversimplified example, it is like thinking, "All successful businessmen in the past have had handlebar mustaches. If I become successful in business, I will need to grow a handlebar mustache. But I'm a girl and I don't think that will look good on me, so maybe I don't want to be successful in business."

So in order to feel comfortable achieving business success, you will need to reframe your paradigm. You could re–imagine business success to look the way you like, whether that includes a 'stache or not. Perhaps your version of a successful businessperson could included "Passion Red" lipstick, or black lipstick and a tongue piercing. Or cargo shorts and a T–shirt instead of a suit. Your paradigm for what success looks like does not need to match anyone else's.

Here are a few more oversimplified examples, "All cops are serious and @ssholes, so I need to be just as serious and bad @ss as the rest of them." Or, "All novelists are incredibly well read. So unless I have read all the classics, I should forget about being an author." Or, "I'm a Republican, so I am anti–abortion." Or, "I'm a Democrat, so I just want to tax the rich." These are stereotypes and generalizations and are going to do no one any good.

> **SSN–The Limitations of Labels (SSN)**
> http://bit.ly/SSN-Labels

Lets look at a more complex, real-life example. My friend Quinn has been in a loving relationship with his live–in girlfriend, Suzy, for over ten years. He loves her, but cannot bring himself to ask her to marry him. They currently live their lives the way most married couples live, so it's fair to assume that he doesn't object to the lifestyle.

Based on our conversations, we've determined that he has a paradigm about what marriage is going to be like. He is enjoying the way things are going as boyfriend/girlfriend, but thinks if he gets married, he is suddenly going to have to be home each night at 5:00, that he will have to start a family right away, that he will have to stop going to see live music (which he loves), etc. He fears something about his paradigm regarding marriage. But marriage, as we have talked about before, does not have to include the bogeymen he fears. Their marriage can be whatever Suzy and Quinn desire, as long as they are both in agreement.

Instead of focusing on what he "knows" marriage is supposed to be like, he can re–imagine a future and a marriage that functions in a way that makes them both happy.

A paradigm about how life is "supposed to be" is merely an OPTION as to how life could be, but there are endless options as to how your life can look. Imagine the possibilities and find the ideas that fit YOU.

"Be who you are and say what you feel, because those who mind don't matter and those who matter don't mind."
– Dr. Seuss

Takeaway: Your life can be and function the way you want it to. Your life does not need to resemble anyone else's life.

Reminder From Previous Sidenote: So, who are you? Why are you here? What is the meaning to this life anyway? Be who you is!

What past hurt are you projecting onto the future?

When I talk about past hurt being projected onto the future, I am referring to the "well, from what I've seen, this always ends badly, so why even try" attitude. Remind yourself that each situation you are in is unique. All too often you take your past hurts, and the hurts that you have seen others go through, and project them onto this new unique situation. Have you ever heard yourself say, "Things are going well, but every time I start to really like a guy/girl, something always goes wrong and we end up breaking up." Or, "I never get the job I really want, especially when I really want it." Or, "I've dealt with (insert whatever ethnicity, gender, sexuality here) in the past. You can't trust them." When you say things like this, you are taking past hurts and projecting them onto this new, unique situation.

When you do this, you are not being fair to the situation, or the person, you are dealing with. The person or situation before you is not the same person or situation that you encountered in the past. Instead of just reacting and giving up because, "trying ___ never works." Focus on the PRESENT situation. This present situation could go your way. Keep in mind, that if it does work out, you are going to be in an unknown place, but that does not mean that it is not safe.

Take what you have learned from your past experience and use it to make this new situation even better. Don't use the past as an excuse to not act.

For instance, the next time I start a business with a friend, I will have a buy/sell agreement in place from beginning. I learned my lesson. Without having a buy/sell agreement in place, I had a business arrangement ended very badly. The bad experience I had won't stop me from trying to start a new business with a friend but it will make me act smarter with the next business.

What happened in the past is past. Each situation is unique. You are not doomed to repeat your past hurts every time. Learn from them, but never let them stop you from taking risks in the future.

"If we listened to our intellect, we'd never have a love affair. We'd never have a friendship. We'd never go into business, because we'd be cynical. Well, that's nonsense. You've got to jump off cliffs all the time and build your wings on the way down."
—Ray Bradbury

Takeaway: The past is past. Learn from it, but consider each situation in its uniqueness and act and risk accordingly.

Are you really a "victim" of your circumstances?

Being a victim of your circumstances is just another way to stay safe. After all, isn't it soooo much easier to blame someone else for your problems than take responsibility for your situation? Isn't it? "My husband won't let me." "Society doesn't accept people like me." "Nobody is hiring right now." "Nobody is buying right now." "I just don't have time to date." etc. etc. etc. UGHHH! If you are handing out an excuse, you are playing the victim and keeping yourself in the safe zone.

Perhaps you desire to be in a romantic relationship. Most likely, that means you need to start dating. You want to look your best, so you decide to lose a little weight, but you can't seem to drop more than two pounds before you gain back five. You think if you lose 20 pounds you will look more desirable, and you can fulfill your conscious desire to have a loving companion in your life, but subconsciously you are a little scared that if you find someone, you are going to get your heart stomped on again. Part of you wants to stay safe and not risk the POSSIBLE hurt that may result from loving someone else. What better way to stay safe than to not reach your goal of losing weight? Then you never have to feel ready (worthy) to date. Then you can blame the fact that you are not dating on the excuse that all men want impractically skinny supermodels, blah, blah, blah. You get to play the victim.

Look again at the example above. What is the character really doing? He or she is:

- •Projecting past hurts on the present. Just because you had your heart broken in the past does not mean that it will happen this time. It only takes one time to start a lifelong relationship.
- •Avoiding the worst case scenario. Seriously, what's the worst that could happen? (See Part 2, Chapter 4 – "What's the worst that can happen if the worst that can happen, happens?")
- • Not feeling worthy of their desires. People are beautiful in every shape and size. Everyone is worthy of a loving relationship.
- • Thinking they need to do X before they do Y. People date and love at any size. You do not need to be supermodel skinny to date and find love. (See the Part 2, Chapter 6 – "Welcome Struggles" for more on this topic.)

So, stop doing all those things! You do not need to be a victim! You are just keeping yourself safe by making up excuses. Stop making excuses and start living the life you want! You are only a victim if you CHOOSE to be.

Victims give away their power. If you make yourself a victim, you are powerless and you are stuck in your sameness. If you know that you are not a victim, which you are not, then you can unscribble your problem. Take control over your life and be happy knowing you are working to fulfill your desires.

You never have to think of yourself as a victim. If something bad happens in your life, acknowledge that it happened and move forward from there. Unscribble your way back to where you want to be.

The other day I was watching football. The commentators were discussing how easily one of the quarterbacks took every setback of the game in stride. He'd get sacked, then jump back up and got ready for the next play. He did not get mad or sad, he just got back up and tried again. The commentator added that when the quarterback was interviewed, he said he learned this get–back–up ability by watching his parents. Whenever something bad would happen, his dad or mom would say, "Okay..." (as in, "crap!") "Okay..." (as in, "this is where we are") "Okay..." (as in, "time to move forward"). Then they would ask, "Now what?" and explore where to go from there. With each "okay," you could feel a shift to acceptance of the situation, then to an attitude of moving forward.

How BRILLIANT! If they were ever "victims" that feeling lasted for about three seconds; as long as it took them to accept the situation as it was and start to look forward again. The next time you feel like a victim, just say, "Okay (crap!)... Okay (this is where we are)... Okay (time to move forward)." Accept how things are and unscribble yourself forward. (See Part 2, Chapter 7 – "Changing Your Attitude" for more on this topic.)

"What does responsibility mean? Responsibility means not blaming anyone or anything for your situation, including yourself. Having accepted this circumstance, this event, this problem, responsibility then means the ability to have a creative response to the situation as it is now. All problems contain the seeds of opportunity, and this awareness allows you to take the moment and transform it to a better situation or thing."
–Deepak Chopra

Takeaway: If you are making excuses and playing the victim, you are keeping yourself in sameness – in other words, safe. Accept your situation as it is and then get yourself back on track by unscribbling a new path toward realizing your dreams and desires.

⬛ **SSN – Responsibility versus victim**
http://bit.ly/SSN-Responsibility

Are you afraid of failing?

It has to be one of the most obvious reasons to avoid the big scary future that you have imagined. Everyone fails at something at some point in their lives. If you never fail at anything, you are not risking enough. Failing is not a bad thing, it's a learning experience. (See Part 2, Chapter 6 –"Welcome Struggles") Prepare yourself as much as you can to facilitate success, but if you fail, learn from your failure and try again. (Be sure to read the upcoming chapter "What's the Worst that can Happen" – Part 2, Chapter 4 – to delve deeper into this subject.)

> *"When defeat comes, accept it as a signal that your plans are not sound, rebuild those plans, and set sail once more toward your coveted goal."*
> *–Napoleon Hill*

Takeaway: Failure is nothing but a learning experience.

Are you intimidated by the bigness of your desires?

Sometimes when you think of something you want to do, you imagine it in its entirety; in its largeness; in its allness. That can feel intimidating, and make you want to stick your head in the sand and do nothing. But if you reverse–bubble it down to manageable steps, it won't feel that scary.

Remember, you don't have to create ALL of the parts of your desire at once. Just start by taking that first baby step. Rome wasn't built in a day. The Romans had their eyes on the prize, but took one small step after another to achieve greatness.

Take it from Shel Silverstein's poem about Melinda Mae, who ate a monstrous whale. "She took little bites and she chewed very slow... and in eighty–nine years she ate that whale." She started with a little bite from the tail.

Where can you start? Reverse-bubble things back to a point where that first step doesn't feel scary, then dig in and get to work. Eventually, by tackling it bit by bit, you'll fulfill your desire.

"Be not afraid of going slowly; be afraid only of standing still."
—Chinese Proverb

Takeaway: You don't have to take on the "all" of a project. Reverse-bubble things back from your solution and find that first step. Then take it step by step.

Are you just procrastinating?

Procrastination literally means, "to defer an action; to put off until another day or time; defer; delay." But if you keep saying, "I'll do it tomorrow." It's just another way of giving in to those darn bogeymen. If you really desire something, stop procrastinating! It will NEVER be the perfect time to start anything. If you want you can find an excuse to not do things for the rest of your life.

But your unknown future, full of treasure, is waiting for you if you have the courage to open that closet door and face your bogeymen. First accept the situation as it is, then work through the unscribbling process:
  • Become aware of your desires.
  • Set your intentions.
  • Brainstorm solutions that fit into your current situation.
  • Decide on an option to explore while keeping yourself open to new ideas.
  • Explore your solution and reverse-bubble how to get to a point where you can take action.

- Take action.
- Thank.

But whatever you do, take action! Staying safe is not going to help you realize your desires. The future does not have to be scary or the way you imagined it. As you strive for your desires, your life will change. But isn't that what you want with your desires? To feel and experience something you aren't right now? Remember, you ARE safe. You know how to problem solve and unscribble, and because of this you can handle anything that is thrown at you. You will be fine. Experience and explore the new. Take action now!

> *"Things may come to those who wait,*
> *but only the things left by those who hustle."*
> *– Abraham Lincoln*

Takeaway: If you are procrastinating, you are just keeping yourself safe and avoiding the unknown future – good or bad.

Unknown does not mean unsafe. The unknown could actually be wonderful. But you won't get to explore any of it if you don't take action.

P.S. Matthew Ferry does some great lectures on what he calls our "Drunk Monkey" mind that works and works to keep us "safe" even when there is no danger. I highly recommend you check out some of his teachings if you feel you are stuck trying to stay safe. http://www.matthewferry.com

SSN– Matthew Ferry on the Drunk Monkey
http://bit.ly/SSN-DrunkMonkey

And remember…

> *"If you play it safe in life you've decided*
> *that you don't want to grow any more."*
> *—Shirley Hufstedler*

Keep growing!

What's the worst that can happen if the worst that can happen happens?

Fear often paralyzes us from taking steps to fulfill our desires. But realistically, what's the worst that could happen if you take a step? When you are faced with deciding whether or not to go forward with an action, ask yourself, "What's the worst that can happen if the worst that can happen happens?" If you can survive that, it's probably not so bad to take action, is it?

So, what's the worst that can happen?

Someone might laugh at you?

We've all done stupid things at times. Don't take life (or yourself) so seriously. If you can learn to laugh at yourself while everyone is laughing at you – people will actually like you even more.

A bunch of my friends were out bowling. It was Marcus' turn to bowl. He stepped up, and started to do his fancy footwork before releasing the ball. In the process, he tripped on his own feet. Naturally, we all started laughing. It's just too hard not to laugh at physical comedy. Instead of being embarrassed, Marcus went with it – exaggerating his fall, letting himself fall on his stomach and his legs fly up in the air behind him – making us all laugh even harder. His ability to laugh at himself turned an embarrassing moment into one that made him a more endearing and fun friend to be around.

When people are laughing at you, take the opportunity to laugh along with them.

"Through humor, you can soften some of the worst blows that life delivers. And once you find laughter, no matter how painful your situation might be, you can survive it."
– Bill Cosby

Takeaway: Learn to laugh at yourself. Life is funny, and sometimes we do funny things.

You might have to admit that you made a mistake?

There is nothing worse then having to admit you are wrong, is there? It means you have to admit that you are not perfect. Well guess what – NO ONE IS PERFECT! We all make mistakes.

Your mistake is just a learning experience. Within every mistake there is a bit of knowledge to be learned. You just learned that whatever way you were going about things is not the best way. Perfect. Now that you have eliminated that solution you can try another way. How do you think inventions are created? Trial and error. Trial and error. Trial and error. It's the same with life. You don't have to get it perfect right out of the gate. Life is trial and error, and it is important to learn and try things in different ways until you find one that works for you. Embrace your failures; they are leading you to a BETTER way.

Life is like a giant science experiment. Keep trying things. Make adjustments and try again. Eventually you will figure things out. So if you were wrong about something, who cares? Make adjustments or atonements and move on.

"The difference between greatness and mediocrity is often how an individual views a mistake..."
— Nelson Boswell

Takeaway: Everyone makes mistakes. Learn from them and move on.

You might die?

Really, how often are you going to put yourself in a situation that could be life threatening?

Sure, if you tell a waiter he screwed up the bill, there is a slight chance that he is emotionally unstable and will stab you with a steak knife, but what are the odds of that? Seriously?

The worst that can happen in MOST situations is not death. If death is a possibility, FIND ANOTHER SOLUTION, or do the preparation work necessary to decrease the risk. If death is not a serious possibility, then what IS the worst that could happen? Is it that bad? Could you survive it?

We are all going to die sometime. You can't avoid it. So take a few risks and enjoy life. I am not suggesting you put yourself in deliberate danger; seriously, don't do that! But don't forget to live and maybe take a few risks too.

"The question is not whether we will die, but how we will live."
— Joan Borysenko

Takeaway: In MOST situations the worst that might happen is not death. If death is a very real possibility, find a different solution to your problem.

Play the "what's the worst that can happen" game:

This is a fun game you can play when you are reluctant to do something. Ask yourself, "What's the worst that can happen if the worst that can happen happens?" If you find that you can handle the scenario you come up with (and you most likely can), what do you have to lose?

Takeaway: When you are afraid to make a move, ask yourself, "What if the worst that can happen happens?" If you can survive that, go for it!

Side Note: Here is how I learned to play the game, "What's the worst that can happen?"

About 30 minutes before I was expecting some prospective buyers to drop by a condo that I was showing for a friend, the place was suddenly filled with the sounds of ABBA. I mean filled!

"You can dance, you can jive. Having the time of your life. Ooh, see that girl, watch that scene. Dig in the dancing queen."

The downstairs neighbor, who was normally gone on the weekends, was blaring ABBA!! I did not think any potential buyer, even a huge fan like myself, would appreciate hearing ABBA on the whim of a neighbor! Pacing the condo (in socks, mind you) I waited, hoping the music would stop.

15 minutes went by. I started to think that I was going to have to ask him to turn it down. I said to myself, "Just go ask him! It's no big deal. He's probably friendly. If you ask nicely, he should understand and turn it down. Right?" But the very thought of asking him scared the crap out of me! I'm from

the Midwest – we avoid conflict at all costs! "Maybe if I wait a little bit longer it will stop," I told myself.

10 minutes before arrival time....

"If you're all alone when the pretty birds have flown. Honey I'm still free. Take a chance on me."

"Damn it! I have to do this." Taking a deep breath, I mustered up the courage, put my shoes on and walked downstairs. I knocked on the door and waited. No answer. "I know he's home," I thought. I knocked again, this time louder, in case he couldn't hear me over the "Honey I'm still free. Take a chance on me." I heard him come to the door, but the door did not open. He walked away.

Okay, now I'm getting annoyed! In seven minutes, I'm going to lose a prospective buyer. So I knocked even louder. The door opened.

In my sweetest voice, I said, "Hi, I'm upstairs. I have someone coming to look at the condo in about five minutes. I was wondering if you would turn your music down for maybe 15 minutes."

As I was trying to finish with a smile, he simply answered, "No," and shut the door before I could even register what he said.

No? Did he just say "No"? Who says that? Who would do that? What the "F" is his problem? I asked nicely!

After trying unsuccessfully to get an answer when I knocked again, I stomped upstairs. Dude has another thing coming if he wants to pick a noise fight with the person upstairs. I have CLOGS!

After opening a few windows to let in some street noise, and talking as much as I could to distract the focus from the "Mamma mia, here I go again. My my, how can I resist you," the potential buyers left. I was thankful that no one mentioned the music.

As I tried to resist stomping around the apartment, it occurred to me that the worst thing I had imagined happening had happened. He said, "no" and shut the door in my face, and...

I survived.

So if you can, envision the worst that can happen happening, and ask yourself, "Can I survive that?" If you can, go for it! If not, perhaps you need to come up with a different solution. One where you could survive if the worst that could happen happens.

"Anything I've ever done that ultimately was worthwhile...
initially scared me to death."
– Betty Bender

"Accept that all of us can be hurt, that all of us can—and surely
will at times—fail. I think we should follow a simple rule: if we
can take the worst, take the risk"
–Joyce Brothers

Co–unscribbling

When you are in a relationship, family, business, organization or any entity that involves more than just you, involve as many people as you can, as early as you can, in the unscribbling process. Especially involve any key players who will be affected by the steps necessary to fulfill the desire. When you involve others, it helps create a shared passion for the desire, keeps everyone engaged in active solution finding, and keeps everyone rowing the boat in the same direction.

When you can't involve everyone in the unscribbling process, it is still good to let anyone helping you in the pursuit of your desires know as much about the overall plan as you can. Explain to them:

- What the ultimate desire/intention of the project is.
- Why you chose the solution you chose.
- The plan and steps to get there.
- Then ASK for their involvement where needed.

If they agree to help you, explaining your logic allows them to share in your vision and enthusiasm to achieve your desire. They need to be able to see the full view in order to buy in to your plan. Unless they see your full vision, you will likely be met with reluctance, apathy or even hostility, which will not help you get closer to your desires.

Let's look at a couple of scenarios:

1. Family

The Smith family has the shared desire to increase the level of fulfillment Mom feels. Because of this, Dad might volunteer to cook dinner three nights a week so she can go back to school those nights. Jenny and Johnny might be more willing to do a few chores around the house so Mom can study. When the family knows the desire – for Mom to be more fulfilled in life – and they have agreed that the best solution is for her to go back to school and get a master's degree, they can clearly understand how to contribute. It might help to explain that Mom can then get a higher paying job, and help pay for Jenny and Johnny to go to college someday. A little "what's in it for me" never hurts.

But imagine if Mom decides to go back to school all on her own, without discussing it with her family first. One day she says, "I have an announcement. I am going to go back to school to get my masters degree. Dad, I need you to get home from work a tad earlier three days a week so you can make dinner. Kids, I need you to start doing your own laundry." Oh, can you imagine the reaction? Most likely the reaction would be anger, resentment, resistance and maybe even a temper tantrum or two.

2. Business

A recession has hit, profits are down and it's time to unscribble. You sit down with your management team, clarify your desire to keep the company viable or growing, then brainstorm ideas and possibilities with them on how to make that happen. By opening the process of unscribbling to all involved, you may discover cost saving methods you never imagined. You may have an employee step up and say, "I've been thinking our product might be good for a new target market." Or, "What if we went solar?" Or, "What if we create a new service add–on to offer our customers?"

Can you imagine if, instead of co–unscribbling with your team, you look at the numbers and announce that everyone will receive a 10 percent pay cut indefinitely. What happens? Now Steve, who was thinking about approaching the company with his new target market idea, gets annoyed. "What? I've been working my ass off for five years, and now you tell me that you're going to CUT my pay?

Why? So the owner can keep his fancy boat? Screw this company! I'm going to strike out on my own with my idea." Now you've lost a valuable employee and a possible BETTER solution!

3. Dare I say... Government?

Wow, this one is tricky and I think it speaks a lot to perceived intentions.

We are a government, "for the people, by the people," searching for the best ways to allow everyone the ability to pursue "life, liberty and the pursuit of happiness." Basically, and this is my assumption, I think the core desire of the nation comes down to wanting to live in peace and harmony.

So, ask yourself, do you perceive your politicians, as they are trying to balance the budget, thinking:

"We desire to live in peace and harmony. Because of this, we intend to create a balanced budget, so that all whom we engage with will feel fairly treated, both the tax payers as well as those we employ to do the services of the country. What ways can we find to keep the government working and increase efforts to expand the overall peace and harmony of the nation?"

In theory, this is supposed to be how it works. And in defense of our politicians, maybe this is what is happening. But does it feel like this is the desire the politicians keep in mind as they are tackling problems? Or do you think there are other desires being pursued? Even if there are not, if you (as someone who will be involved in the steps to carry out any plans set forth), if you think there MIGHT be other desires being pursued, how will you feel about paying higher taxes? How happily will you pitch in and metaphorically do the laundry? How happily will you do ANYTHING without knowing the core desire that is trying to be fulfilled?

Wouldn't it be great if we saw the full unscribbling exercise of every politician's desires? Wouldn't it be great if we could really see why they are making their decisions? Wouldn't it be great to say, "I get it. I see what you are going after. Great ideas! How can I help?"

In any situation, with any kind of group, it's important that everyone knows what your true desires and intentions are in order for them to feel compelled to participate in making them happen. If whatever you are unscribbling involves other people, please, get as many people involved in the process as you can. Or, make it clear what the core desires are, and why you chose the solution you did, and then ASK them to participate.

When the vision behind a desire and the reasoning behind the steps are clear, understood and shared by all involved, amazing things can happen. How often have you explained something to someone only to have him exclaim, "Oh, now I see!" Once the vision becomes clear, the co–unscribblers bubble with excitement; they see how they can help, and they might even suggest better ways for you to accomplish your intention. When they can see why the plan exists and how the plan lays out, they can make it their own and they can share in what Steven Covey calls, "the passion of vision." When they share in your vision and see what you are striving for, they feel empowered and enthusiastically help you to achieve your desires. Your desires become theirs.

With a shared passion for the vision, all involved will become empowered with purpose. But that won't happen as easily if you just tell someone what you want him or her to do.

I have found that when I don't involve people in the unscribbling process, and instead present ideas and plans without their input, two things happen:

1. They instinctively reject the idea.
2. They ignore it, hoping it will go away on its own. This is especially true of any action or plan that involves them directly. I usually get that, "OKAY, I think you are bit crazy" look as they walk away.

I can't blame anyone for this reaction; I react the same way when someone gets bossy with me. There is something about being told what to do that people resent. And if bossy–pants insists on getting her way and tells people what to do and exactly how to do it, the results are anything but productive. When you imagined the scenarios we discussed earlier, where people were told of solutions without being part of the unscribbling, in your imagination, did you see:

> The people involved start to mentally and emotionally shut down?
> - Family – the family members slumping at the table?
> - Business – the employees retreating into their own thoughts and worries?
> - Government – the voter becoming apathetic and NOT voting?

> Some people becoming outright hostile (or passive–aggressive, which is still hostility)?
> - Family –Johnny acting out and getting in trouble at school, or Dad "forgetting" he needed to come home early to make dinner?
> - Business – your team no longer giving 100 percent, or people stealing office supplies, or leaving early?
> - Government – people protesting?

> Them stop CONTRIBUTING. Why should they? If they don't know what they are doing or why, if you aren't allowing them to help you formulate the plan, and you aren't listening to their advice, why should they?
> - Family–Dad suddenly deciding to play golf more, because if Mom can take time for herself, why can't he?
> - Business – employees mentally working on their resumes and planning their exits, or looking for a job where someone will listen to them and value their opinion?
> - Government – people stop listening to the news and watch reality TV instead?

But if you co–unscribble, listen to everyone's input, and get agreement on the vision and the actions needed to achieve it – look out! With a shared vision and unscribbling skills, your "co" will be unstoppable.

P.S. I realize that in the case of government it is more complicated than it looks, but hopefully you get the point I am trying to demonstrate.

"If you want to build a ship, don't drum up people together to collect wood and don't assign them tasks and work, but rather teach them to long for the endless immensity of the sea"
– Antoine de Saint–Exupery

Takeaway: Involving others in the Unscribbling process will help to create a shared vision and passion.

Ask for others to participate in your vision

People love to help one another when they are asked, not told what to do. If you have independently worked the unscribbling process, then at the least ask anyone who is affected by the decision if they are willing to be involved.

Change, "I'm going to need you to _____." to "Would you be willing to _____?" If they say no, unscribble another way to accomplish your plan. Do not, under any circumstances, force someone to participate in helping you to reach your desires.

Let's look at Mom again from the previous example. If she sits down with her husband and says, "Hon, I've really been feeling unfulfilled at work. I've been thinking about going back to school and getting my masters degree. I think if I do that, I'll be able to get a job teaching at the university. I feel like I could really make a difference as a teacher. What do you think? Do you think you could get home a little earlier a few days a week to make dinner for the kids?"

Approaching another and getting their input will take you far! Even if Dad said, "Sweetie, I wish I could, but Tracy is out on family medical leave for the next three months." NO PROBLEM! Why? You know how to unscribble! Keep the conversation going forward with, "I understand. Is there some other solution that we can come up with so I can take this class?" DAMN STRAIGHT there is! And now you have two people looking for solutions! How great is that?

By asking other people to participate, you either get them on board with you rowing one of the oars, or you get them to help you to find another rower. Ask for participation and you will be amazed at how happily people will help you.

People want to be included. I've actually heard stories of friendships "breaking up" because one party wasn't accepting help from the other! They want to help. Just ask, you will be amazed.

"To me it seems that to give happiness is a far nobler goal that to attain it: and that what we exist for is much more a matter of relations to others than a matter of individual progress: much more a matter of helping others to heaven than of getting there ourselves."
– Lewis Carroll

Takeaway: If you want others to willingly help you achieve your desires, you must ask them to participate.

In resistance are the seeds of more desires

If, while you are co–unscribbling, you run into a big "but" type of person, take a moment to look at their "but" before you dismiss them as uncooperative. For in their "but" is another desire, or a way to clarify what the true desire is. (Wow, does that sound wrong! Forgive me for this one too, please.)

Let's look at our example of the company looking for ways to remain viable. One of the managers suggests, "We could go after a new target market, BUT then we need to advertise, and that costs money. We need to save money, not spend money." This "but" can help you clarify your desire. Remember, you know how to get butless – find the hidden desire in the but. Add this new desire as a clarifier to your desire, or unscribble it on its own. So, now the desire may become, "We desire to be a viable and growing business while being as cost effective as we can be."

I would argue that advertising is a solution to the question

"How do we approach a new target market?" During the initial brainstorming, this is thinking one step too far. Try to keep your buts out until you get to the phase where you are deciding on a solution to explore.

However, if someone can't resist, listen to them and clarify your desire, or ask them to write it down so it is considered later when you are narrowing down the possible solutions. Whether you clarify right away, or hold it to the vetting stage, the "but" contains insight, and will help you choose a solution to explore. Perhaps you stay with "reaching out to a new target market," but when exploring the "how do we?" part of the brainstorming, you are able to come up with more cost effective solutions than advertising.

The point is, in the "but" there may be a clarifier that will help you down the road. To ignore the "but" will do two things:

1. Annoy the "but" person, making him shut down, get hostile, or stop contributing. And/or:
2. You might overlook a necessary qualifier to your desire that will help in the problem solving process.

By listening and acknowledging, you have kept the person open, thinking and contributing solutions. You have also helped focus the group's thinking.

I recently designed a postcard for my client, My Charmed Life (MCL). They sell charms and charm bracelets. (Love this client! Be sure to check them out at www.mycharmedlife.com) The postcard was to be handed out to attendees at a sorority event. The objective was to promote MCL and distribute a charm, which was attached as a gift for the attendees. We created a piece that fit the MCL branding and met all of our other desires. When MCL showed the design to the event coordinator, she said, "BUT the theme is rock star oriented, so the postcard should be edgier looking." Okay. That would have been a good "but" to know earlier, but we progressed.

We created a new design that fulfilled all our old desires as well as the new desires. This time the event coordinator said, "BUT now it's too edgy. We have alumni coming to this event and we can't look that edgy!" Okay... So edgy, but not. Got it. With this clarification, the third design hit the mark.

Had we heard all those "buts" at the beginning of the process we would have saved ourselves a lot of time. So, listen to the "but" guy, even if you'd like to tell him where to stick it!

> *"Confront issues and challenges – not each other."*
> *– Suzanne Mayo Frindt*

Takeaway: By acknowledging resistance to solutions you may find ways to clarify your desire or narrow down your solutions.

Your shared vision becomes your mission statement or purpose

A shared vision will empower everyone involved, not just the originator. It can become the group's mission statement, and help them define their purpose and ways of behaving.

There are three main benefits that a mission statement can provide:

1. It helps set the framework for your services and the experience of everyone you encounter.
2. It helps everyone in the company know how to act, no matter what circumstances arise.
3. It allows the "ship" to sail and function if the originator becomes lost at sea.

In one of my previous business arrangement I was a partner in a hair salon in Chicago. (Don't worry, I was not cutting hair.) We decide that our core desire/mission statement/purpose/philosophy would be to build a profitable hair salon that:

– Has world-class, consistent customer service.
– Is relaxed, friendly and fun.
– Provides service and style specific to the individual client's needs.
– Engages in no transaction that does not benefit all whom it affects.

– Works smarter, not harder.

This became the entire salon's mission. Knowing our mission helped us to shape every experience that our customers could have had in or in regards to the salon. With any possible idea we came up with for services, marketing or behavior we could ask ourselves:
  – Does this help us provide world-class, consistent customer service?
  – Does this help us maintain a relaxed, friendly and fun feel?
  – Does this help us provide service and style specific to each client's needs?
  – Do our transactions benefit all whom they affect?
  – Does this help us works smarter, not harder?

This mission also helped any employees know how to act if a manager was not present. They can ask themselves the questions above and respond accordingly.

Having a shared vision also allows for the mission to live as the cast of characters changes. I left the salon, but the salon lived and still thrives without me. My ego would have liked to have seen it wither without me, but if you build a business with a strong base, it becomes its own entity. So I am proud that it is still thriving without me. We set it up right. We set it up to live despite changes. (Well, that, and I must admit my ex–business partner does amazing hair and busts his ass to make it successful.)

A collective shared vision/desire/mission statement can empower an idea by helping the group work together toward the same purpose. Make sure everyone in your organization or group knows the core desires.

"Without mission, there's no purpose. Without vision, there's no destination. Without values, there are no guiding principles."
– Paul B. Thornton

Takeaway: Let your core desires help you form your group's mission, vision and actions.

Side Note: Don't tell people what to do; encourage them to explore solutions

I know it is cliché that when women discuss an issue they are facing, they get frustrated when the man they're talking to tells them what to do to solve the problem.

The woman will often reply, "Please don't TELL me what to do. I am just talking. You are just supposed to be listening." This tends to thoroughly confuse men, as when they discuss an issue it is typically because they are looking for an answer.

Well, it is so cliché that I think it is worth exploring. It's not just a women versus men way of communicating. I've seen women do the telling and I've seen men get frustrated by being told what to do. And the arguments discussed above are both wrong in my eyes.

As we have talked about before, nobody likes being told what to do. So men (or women) who do this, stop telling people what they should do. NEVER say, "You should do X." Or, even the toned-down version, "If I were you I would Y." These answers limit the brainstorming by declaring the best solution before you even get a chance to brainstorm and explore. Worse yet, it assuming the person discussing the issue hasn't already considered this solution, which is patronizing.

But women are wrong to say that they are not looking for solutions. They are, they just want them presented differently. (I mean really, if someone just sat there and nodded as they talked, not giving any kind of response, that would make them angry too.)

So, men, don't TELL women what to do. If you phrase your ideas in the form of a question you will get a lot further and help move the conversation forward. For instance say, "Have you thought about Z?" versus "You should Z." Or, "What if you tried X?" versus, "If I were you, I'd X."

By phrasing it in a question you keep the dialogue open. You haven't assumed that she has not already considered your solution. So you haven't patronized her.

Plus, this allows her to talk and clarify her desire. If you ask, "Have you considered option D?" She can come back with her "but" – "Yes, but we need Q and T too." Perfect, now you have a clearer picture of the true desire. Now you can brainstorm for that newly clarified desire.

"Men and women belong to different species, and communication between them is a science still in its infancy."
– Bill Cosby

Takeaway: When someone presents you with a problem, help them brainstorm and clarify their true desire by asking them if they have considered different solutions instead of telling them what you think they should do.

Welcome struggles

As I mentioned before, most people do not welcome struggles in their lives. But remember, bad feelings are actually here to help you. They are emotional clues telling you to make adjustments in what you are doing.

Once the adjustment is made and you are back on course, you will feel better. To help identify where you need to make an adjustment, return to your unscribbling process. Ask:

- Are you working toward your true desire?
- Do you need to tweak your chosen solution or methodology?
- Are you stuck on one way to accomplish your desire? Do you need to find another solution?
- Are you resisting a better solution?
- Have you reverse-bubbled your vision back to an appropriate step for you at this moment?
- Has your desire changed? (See Part 2, Chapter 9 titled "Desires Change")

We will talk more about each of these areas throughout this chapter.

When we look at our struggles as signals, they become opportunities in disguise. They are clues to make adjustments and possibly take our lives in a new direction.

"Pain is inevitable; suffering is optional"
— Peggy Bassett

Takeaway: Struggles, or negative feelings, are clues from your internal emotional guidance system suggesting you make an adjustment.

Are you working towards your true desire?

Sometimes life feels like a struggle when you are working towards solutions that don't fit your true desires. Make sure you are focused on your true desire and are not getting sidetracked by things you think you are supposed to be doing instead. Let's break it down a little bit more.

1. Are you pursuing solutions that are the best fit for your personality/situation or because you are "supposed to?"
   Are you trying to bring your company public when you really like running it mom and pop style? Are you striving for a management position at your company, when you really don't like managing people? Are you trying to date the hottie two cubicles down even though she never gets your jokes?

2. Are you stuck on the thought that there is a hard and fast order to how you are "supposed to" do things in your life? Do you feel like you need to make a lot of money and retire before you can see the world? Do you want to pursue a different career, but feel you need to wait until your kids are out of the house? Do you want to have kids, but feel you need to be married first? Ask yourself, do I HAVE to do X before I am able to do Y? Or is there another way for me to be able to do Y? (P.S. There is ALWAYS another way.)

These "supposed to's" are nothing more than peer pressure gone amuck. Gone amuck, because no one actually told you that you HAD to do things such and such a way. (If they did, tell them to go fly a kite.) There is nothing in this life that you are supposed to do or supposed to want. Nothing. There are only OPTIONS of things you CAN do, but nothing you HAVE to do. Your life is meant to be what you desire it to be.

Just because everyone else is smoking dope, drinking, getting married, having kids, taking a corporate job, playing golf, organizing gigantic birthday parties for their kids, buying people expensive holiday gifts, etc., does not mean YOU have to! Or, to quote my mom, "If everyone else was jumping off a cliff would you too?" (Man, did I hate hearing that growing up, but darn it if she wasn't right!) Oftentimes, we strive for things in our lives because we think those are the things we are supposed to strive for: the big house, the fancy car, the 2.5 kids, the smokin' hot wife, the latest trendy clothes, the management position, the corporate job with all the perks... we are supposed to want all of those things, right? Maybe. But those are just OPTIONS. There is nothing wrong with any of them, if that is truly what you desire. But if they are not a fit for you, don't pursue them! Stay true to what is best for you. Who cares if it isn't what everyone else thinks you are supposed to be doing! Your life is uniquely yours. What works for one does not work for all.

Don't do ANYTHING simply because you are "supposed" to. Remember to "be who you is" and follow your unique life path. (See the Sidenote "So, who are you? Why are you here? What is the meaning of this life anyway?" in Section 1, Step 1)

"Don't ask what the world needs. Ask what makes you come alive, and go do it. Because what the world needs is people who have come alive."
–Howard Thurman

Takeaway: Make sure the desires you pursue and the ways you are pursuing them are the correct match for you, and that you are not doing things because you feel you are supposed to do them.

Do you need to tweak your chosen solution or methodology?

Sometimes you need to tweak the solution you are pursuing. On the road to pursuing your chosen solution, you will naturally gain more knowledge about what you are trying to accomplish and the way you are going about getting it. Keep tweaking your chosen solution and methodology to match your new knowledge. Remember, you are just exploring a solution. Instead of being stuck on ONE way, experiment with your solutions (life) instead.

Think of it as a science experiment. While you are conducting your experiment, you may be thinking Solution A is going to work, but once you start boiling Solution A, you decide that is not quite right; it is producing a terrible odor and turning brown – not at all what you intended. No problem. You learned that A, on its own, does not work. Now you are one step closer to finding a way that does work. Time to tweak and try a new way. So you add a little Solution B and boil your new mixture. You get the reaction you were looking for (at least the stink is gone), but you think you might be able to make it even better by adding a bit of Solution C too, and maybe even taking out a bit of A. Now you are getting some results! It is turning a beautiful blue and smells yummy! Life can be like that too. You may need to experiment, explore and add or subtract to the solution you've chosen to explore to make it the perfect solution for you.

So even if you have developed a solution to start exploring or pursuing, keep clarifying and adjusting. Decide on an initial solution to explore then experiment – you test and try it out; evaluate the results; use the results to set new clarified intentions; test and try again; evaluate again and repeat until you are thrilled with your results.

Dating is a perfect place to experiment and find the right combination for you. I read an article once that suggested writing down 100 characteristics: personality traits, talents, interests and even physical features that you were looking for in your potential partner/lover/companion/suitor – whichever you are intending for your life. Once you know what you're looking for, it's much easier to spot good possible matches when you meet them. Just keep your eyes open for good matches. When I first tried this, I think I initially could only came up with about 30 characteristics. Then I started dating. (I had the basis for my first experiment.)

Here's how my dating experiment progressed. First, I found Joe. (All names have been changed to protect the innocent.) He seemed like a perfect fit. After dating Joe I decided I did like him, but it wasn't going to work. I added to my list, "Someone who actually likes me back." Then, I found Kevin. He fit almost all of the traits on my list, and seemed to like me back, but he was a bit negative. So I added to the list, "Someone who is generally happy and enjoys life." (It is no fun hanging out with someone who is always pointing out negative things.) Then I met Paul, and I added, "Someone who is a good kisser." (He had stiff lips and way too much tongue.) After Jeremy I added, "smells good." (Seriously, he was one odd smelling guy!) You get the point. With each new guy, I was refining and clarifying the solution to my desire to have a loving companion in my life. I had some tears along the way, but I also had a ton of fun. Now, I am married to a guy who fits about 97% of that list, and I am thrilled! The process took time, but helped me get to my perfect solution.

If you truly feel that the solution you're focused on is the best one for you, then embrace each struggle as a learning/clarifying experience; explore, tweak, add to, or subtract from the vision of your solutions and try again. In the introduction to "The Alchemist" by Paulo Coelho he says:

> "The secret to life, though, is to fall seven times
> and to get up eight times."

It's a thought I have often kept in mind when it seemed I would not reach my intentions. With each apparent setback, I told myself, "You just have to get up one more time. This could be the one." This applies to business, dating or whatever.

Look at this science experiment that we call life, and ask yourself:

- What did you learn from your latest attempt?
- How can you tweak what your possible solution looks like?
- How can you try again more intelligently?

"Failure is simply the opportunity to begin again,
this time more intelligently."
–Henry Ford

"Change and growth take place when a person has risked himself and
dares to become involved with experimenting with his own life."
–Herbert Otto

Takeaway: Keep exploring, experimenting with and refining your solution until you get exactly what you want. Test, refine, set your new intentions, explore and repeat.

Are you stuck on one way to accomplish your desire? Do you need to find another solution?

Sometimes you will run into an immovable roadblock – something beyond your control that requires you to switch to a different solution to fulfill your desires. This is where a struggle sometimes feels like a failure.

But where a struggle is a signal, so too is a "failure." It is nothing more than a clue to tell you to make a shift. Go back to your list of possible solutions and explore a new solution.

Remember that failures, mistakes and struggles are nothing more than a learning experience and an opportunity to clarify. So now instead of adding A+B and a little bit of C, we throw out A, B and C and try boiling up some D with a splash of E. And this time we may get a pretty chartreuse that smells like baking cookies! We are still working to fulfill our true desire, we are just taking a different approach.

For many couples, fertility is an issue. There comes a point, after having exhausting ways of having your own biological kids (hormones, in vitro, surrogates, etc.), that you have to consider the possibility you may have just encountered your own immovable roadblock. When this happens, you may need to find another solution to fulfill your desires.

Go back to your desire. If your true desire is "to care for and nurture the next generation," you may want to consider adoption, becoming a foster parent or volunteering with a youth organization. All of these solutions could still fulfill your deeper desire to care and nurture the next generation. It might not be the way you thought you would do it, but these are all ways to fulfill your desire.

Having had two miscarriages at the time of this writing, this is definitely something I have had to think about. For me, the desire behind wanting kids comes down to desiring to feel like I am contributing to something larger and outside of myself. Knowing this, I am free to explore some of the other solutions to achieve this desire. Perhaps I will get involved in Habitat for Humanity. Perhaps I will start volunteering at the hospital again, or start an organization that helps foster kids. I could work to raise money to find a cure for a disease. Or perhaps I will send this book out into the world with the hope it will help someone. All of these solutions would help me fulfill my desire.

So, I have options. Plan A might not be working, so it's time to go to Plan B. There are always other options. Knowing this really does make it okay with me if we can't have kids. (In my case, faith in a higher power helps too.)

If you really want to fulfill your desire, there is always a way. It just might be different from what you originally thought. If Plan A has an immovable roadblock, look at another way to meet your desire. (See also Part 2, Chapter 7 – Change Your Attitude)

"Every day is a new beginning. Treat it that way. Stay away from what might have been, and look at what can be."
–Marsha Petrie Sue

Takeaway: Sometimes it helps to try a different solution to fulfill your desires. If Plan A is not working, try Plan B, or C, or D, or...

Are you resisting a better solution?

Sometimes, while working on a solution, a different one will surface. This is why you should ALWAYS keep yourself open to other solutions in the unscribbling process, and in life. While you are brainstorming solutions, you cannot possibly expect to have enough brain power to come up with EVERY possible solution to fulfill your desires. Nobody could. You can't beat yourself up for this. You just have to stay open to other solutions that appear along the way.

The drug Viagra was developed while Pfizer was looking for a solution to alleviate chest pain in men suffering from angina. However, they discovered that their little blue pill had some other positive side effects on their male test patients – effects that have proven to be MUCH more profitable than chest pain medication. It was not a path they planned to take, but when you see a better solution come out of any "setbacks," it could be good to follow it! Pfizer still developed a useful and profitable pharmaceutical, just not the one they thought they would. (Sidenote: Actually, I know a dog that takes Viagra for a heart condition, so apparently they did alleviate chest pains too. For real, a dog, not a dawg.)

So, anyway – pay attention, and a better solution might be presenting itself to you.

> *"Change is the essence of life. Be willing to surrender what*
> *you are for what you could become."*
> *– Anonymous*

Takeaway: Keep your eyes open to new solutions, even when you are focused on your intended solution. A new and better solution might be present itself to you.

Have you reverse-bubbled your vision back to an appropriate step for you at this moment?

We cannot underestimate the power of being prepared.

Although we want our chosen solution to magically appear the moment we discover that we desire it – we often have to work for it. We need to take our baby steps, one at a time. This is why you take the time to map out and envision the steps to accomplish the solution you have chosen. But you have to make sure you are not working on a step that is "over your head."

There is a TV commercial that demonstrates this well. Picture a man holding a steak knife in one hand and a phone in the other. From the phone, a doctor is giving him directions on how to perform a surgery. At the end of the commercial, the man says, "Shouldn't you be doing this?" This may be an overly simplified example, but the man was not ready to perform surgery. He was not ready for that step. And the doctor who should be performing the surgery did not get to the point where he could cut open another person overnight. He studied and practiced. He took baby steps until he got to a point where he could realize his solution and fulfill his desires. He did not just jump in and start cutting away.

Before you jump into performing surgery, make sure you have taken all the baby steps to make sure you are ready. If the step you are on feels too hard, try breaking it down further to a point where the step is approachable and you feel comfortable working on it. Prepare yourself to undertake one step at a time.

If a step you are working on makes you freeze up, break it down into more manageable steps. Keep breaking it down until you get to a bubble that does not make you want to break out into a cold sweat. Once you get to that, "Okay, I can do that" step, things won't feel like a struggle anymore.

Now take that little step and get on your way, baby!

> "Planning is bringing the future into the present so that
> you can do something about it now."
> –Alan Lakein

Takeaway: Make sure you are on a step in your bubble break-down that you feel comfortable with. If you aren't, keep breaking the steps down until you get there.

SSN – Maybe you're the supporting character in a struggle, not the protagonist?
http://bit.ly/SSN-Protagonist

SSN– The bigger picture of struggles and "Angelic Agitators"
http://bit.ly/SSN-Agitators

Changing your attitude

Sometimes there are circumstances in life that you just can't change – the immovable roadblocks. When that happens, as we discussed in the chapter "Welcome Struggles", look for another way to fulfill your desires. Or, there is another option. You can change your attitude.

Another, less productive choice would be to cry in your beer and complain. But if you really think about it, this probably won't get you anywhere. Complaining only provides temporary relief. If you stay in this mode, you will probably alienate the people around you and miss opportunities to fulfill your desires.

Moving forward after you hit an immovable roadblock can be a miserable journey, or it can be a pleasant and empowering one. The choice is yours. It all comes back to your attitude. After all, your attitude is the one thing in life you CAN control. It might not always feel that way, but you can. In any given moment you can choose to feel annoyed or patient; resistant or accepting; slighted or thankful. Your choice will affect your interactions with others and determine your opportunities in the future.

After all, who wants to be around someone with a bad attitude who complains all the time? Well, maybe other complainers. People who desire to make their lives the best they can be are going to gravitate to people who look to the future, to solutions, to hope. They will not desire to be around people who just cry over the past. And which person are they going to think of and want to work with on their next project? The complainer or the solution finder?

Put the attraction factor to work! (See Sidenote: "When you are empowered, everyone wants you!" in Part 2, Chapter 1 – You are worthy of your desires) If you have a good attitude and focus on solutions, you will be empowered. Empowerment = Confidence. Confidence = Attractive. You will be attractive to potential romantic partners as well as work and business opportunities. More opportunities will be present, resulting in a greater chance that you will find a path/solution to fulfill your desires.

So in your quest to pursue your desires, make sure your attitude is positive and empowered. Create the attraction that will bring about solutions and opportunities.

"You cannot control what happens to you, but you can control your attitude toward what happens to you, and in that, you will be mastering change rather than allowing it to master you."
– Brian Tracy

Takeaway: Bad attitudes are not attractive on anyone. Having a good attitude will create more opportunities and give you a better chance of fulfilling your desires.

Shift into a positive attitude by unscribbling

When you are faced with an unwanted situation, unscribbling it will naturally change your attitude about it! Focus on what you desire. Find a new solution that appeals to you and fulfills your intention. Reverse-bubble yourself to an actionable step (while staying open to new possibilities). Then take action. Do this and you will naturally shift from "woe is me" to empowerment. You have just changed your attitude (and your destiny).

How does unscribbling change your attitude? Let's look at our football player's "Okay. Okay. Okay." statement again. (See "Are you really a 'victim' of your circumstances?" in Part 2, Chapter 3 – Playing it Safe) With each okay, you can:

1. Accept the situation as it is.
2. Unscribble it.

3. Move forward with an empowered attitude.

It is as simple as that.

A friend once called me a "Sunday's Child" and said, "Everything always works out for you." I agree. My life always does work out for me. Why? Because I don't let myself get weighed down by or too disappointed when my Solution A doesn't work. I stay open to those Solution B's and Solution C's. So life always works out, because I always have options. Keeping this in mind helps give me inner peace – at least most of the time. (I am human, after all). At the same time, keeping a good attitude brings me more options. The more pleasant I am, the more people want to help me pursue my desires. They might present me with solutions D, E and F – options I had not even imagined!

Stay positive. Empower yourself by using the unscribbling process. Focus on your intention, NOT the hardships of the situation you might be in. For we tend to move toward where we focus.

"Everything can be taken from a man but one thing: the last of human freedoms – to choose one's attitude in any given set of circumstances, to choose one's own way."
– Viktor Frankl

Takeaway: The fastest way to change your attitude about a problem is to empower yourself by unscribbling it.

Flip your thinking

When all else fails, just change your attitude. Look at the situation, accept it as it is, and "spin" it. Play the politician and spin the story so that everything about it looks and feels like the most perfect thing that could ever have happened.

This can be a little tricky in theory, so let me give you some examples that will help this to make more sense.

1. Cave Kisses

One summer, my sister, my two nephews and I were on a vacation in Kentucky. We decided to go on a guided boat tour of some of the local caves. As the boat entered a cave, one of the girls in the boat let out a little squeal. Some of the condensation from the top of the cave had dripped on her. Not missing a beat, our guide smiled and said, "Oh, you just got a cave kiss! When a drip lands on you, it's the cave's way of kissing you." Instantly everyone wanted to get dripped on! Instead of being "gross," the drops were now desirable. (From disgusting to desired.)

2. Train Station Bar

In Marshfield, Wisconsin there is a bar/restaurant that is located next to working train tracks. So every time a train comes through, conversations are disrupted. This disturbance could be considered a big negative. But instead of being upset with the disruption, the bar owners have turned it into a reason to celebrate! When the train comes through, the bartender rings a bell, everyone cheers, AND they offer 50-cent shots. Instead of, "Oh, that noisy train is so distracting," the business turned it into a party and a profit generator! (From annoyance to something to cheer about.)

3. Separations

Those darn miscarriages can be such a sad thing... unless you change your attitude. (As we discussed in "Am I just stuck on this one way to accomplish my desire" in Part 2, Chapter 6 – Welcome Struggles) Having logically unscribbled the situation and moved forward with my life after my miscarriages, I felt more empowered about the situation, but I still had a lot of sadness about the loss. I discussed this with an energy healer, Dr. Rito Gonzalez, DN, PC. He encouraged me to change my perspective. He suggested instead of feeling sad about the loss, maybe I could focus on the good feelings I had while I was pregnant. Focus, he urged, on the joy those little souls brought for the time they were here. Be thankful for that. The perspective he offered was such a nice way to think about the loss. Focus on the joy, not the sadness with the parting.

As I was talking with my friend, Devon, later that night, he shared with me how sad he was that his girlfriend of three years broke up with him. So I relayed the message from Dr. Rito, that perhaps Devon could be thankful too, for the fun and good times he had with his girlfriend while they were together, instead of being upset that the arrangement had ended.

The same could be said about the death of a loved one. I am not suggesting that one not grieve or mourn when someone you love dies, you go through a divorce, or whatever. But don't stay in that space for too long. If the person who brought you the original joy really loved you, they would not want you to stay sad. They would want to see you happy, striving, and living with your desires fulfilled. We can live the rest of our lives with sadness or we can be thankful for the time and joy we have with whatever souls come our way, for as long as we can have them in our presence. (From sad to grateful.)

4. Relapses are learning experiences

Alcoholics and drug addicts often beat themselves up if they have a relapse. But "up to 80 percent of alcoholics treated for a drinking problem will hit the bottle again at least once." (Psychology Today July/August 2010) Relapse is common, but it does not have to be a catastrophe. The article goes on to say, "The trick is to view the episode of backslide as a chance to learn, an opportunity to develop better techniques for anticipating and avoiding or overcoming urges. This insight applies to a range of problems, from life–threatening drug addictions to compulsions like overeating." (From relapse to learning.)

5. Cancer the "best thing"

While I was interviewing cancer survivor and founder of Imerman Angels (which provides a one–on–one cancer support system), Jonny Imerman said, "You know what? I think, as crazy as it sounds – and Lance Armstrong says the same thing – cancer is the greatest thing that's ever happened to me, that's been forced on me, and it's changed what I do. It's changed how I talk to people. It's changed how we help people... I wouldn't have learned all this stuff. I wouldn't be doing what I'm doing today. I wouldn't be connecting people in the cancer community and helping them if I hadn't gone through it." (From disease to thankful.)

SSN– There are no bad things
http://bit.ly/SSN-NoBad

---

6. Go with it

In Man's Search For Meaning, Viktor Frankl describes a patient who would get nervous and sweat. Excessively sweat. Dr. Frankl advised him to try to sweat more instead of resisting; try to sweat as much as he could when he felt anxious. Guess what? The man stopped sweating when he got nervous. I can't explain this one, but how cool is that trick? Perhaps it has something to do with the thought that, "Whatever you resist will persist and intensify." So when we stop resisting and just go with something, it will go away? (Either way, he went from nervous to... cured!)

7. Get to

In Today We Are Rich by Tim Sanders, he recommends that you change your "have to" list into your "get to" list. That way your task is not a burden, rather it is an opportunity. "I have to walk the dog," becomes, "I get to walk the dog." "I have to go to work," becomes, "I get to go to work." Did you notice that just by changing the way you stated it also changed the way you felt about it? You GET TO walk the dog; other people would love that opportunity. You GET TO go to work; do you realize how many people are out of work and would love to have your job? You get to! (From obligation to opportunity.)

8. Last but not least...

Change your problems into opportunities. When you see problems as opportunities to improve your situation, they become exciting. (From big–scary–thing to new opportunity!)

Changing the way you look at things, spinning them to make yourself feel good about them will help you keep a positive attitude. Spin, baby, spin! It is so much better than the alternative.

"If you don't like something, change it. If you can't change it, change your attitude. Don't complain."
- Maya Angelou

Takeaway: Changing the way you look at things can turn apparent negatives into positives, leaving you with a better more productive attitude.

What we can learn from complaining

Complaining about things without looking for solutions can bring a sense of satisfaction. Otherwise why would we do it? So let's unscribble the act of complaining to find a better way to fulfill the desire that is fulfilled through complaining.

When we bitch and moan, we get people's sympathy and their ATTENTION. That feels good, if we are the complainer; we get a weird energetic lift from venting, even while the listener tends to start feeling crappy. But I would caution, this good feeling will be temporary. Unless the person you are talking with happens to be solution oriented and offers you an option to fulfill your scribbled-up desires, you will be wallowing again before you know it – and no closer to fulfilling your desires.

But we do get an energy lift from complaining. Why? What feelings or experiences do complainers gain from complaining? Maybe we:

- feel loved; when we get sympathy, we feel loved and cared for.
- feel understood and accepted; when our friends join in with the "I know exactly what you mean" we feel understood and accepted.

So instead of complaining, find other ways (solutions) to feel loved, understood and accepted.

The complaining high will be short lived. Complaining will ultimately not help you to fulfill your desires. Think about it. Have you ever been around someone who complains about everything? These people are energy suckers; you end up not wanting to be around them. Their complaining to gain love and acceptance has just backfired!

Had the complainer focused on solutions and told his friend about the situation with a positive attitude, what would happen in the long run? His friends would love being around him because he always has such a good attitude. He would gain the love, acceptance, and support that he craves. AND remember:
- A good attitude and empowerment = confidence
- Confidence = attractive
- Attractive = people want to present you with more opportunities
- More opportunities = a greater chance that you will fulfill your desires

Focus on the intention, NOT the problem. Instead of thinking "poor me," accept the situation as it is, rework the unscribbling process so you can focus on your desired solution, and start on your journey again with a good attitude. Or just change your attitude. People will naturally love, accept and want to understand you.

"The greatest revolution of our generation is the discovery that human beings, by changing the inner attitudes of their minds, can change the outer aspects of their lives."
— William James

Takeaway: Behind a complainer is someone who desires to be loved, understood and accepted. Changing your attitude and focusing on your desired future will bring you more love, understanding and acceptance than complaining.

P.S. Try giving yourself the attention you crave. Take some time to get introspective and look for ways to solve your problem. It's a win–win. You get the attention, and you get your problem solved!

P.P.S. Check out The Celestine Prophecy, by James Redfield, to learn more about how playing the "poor me" card is really your way of controlling others. Veeeery interesting concept. This is a spiritual fiction book, but don't let that sway you. Understanding this concept alone makes the book worth reading, even if you are not spiritual.

SSN– The "Poor Me" drama from the Celestine Prophecy
http://bit.ly/SSN-PoorMe

Point of power

At any given moment, you are in the moment of power. You can choose to complain about the situation, or you can accept it and move forward. You can choose to be sad about things, or find the good. You can choose to wallow or empower yourself. Therefore, you can choose your attitude. In any given moment, you have the power to change your life.

"If you have time to whine and complain about something then you have the time to do something about it."
– Anthony J. D'Angelo, The College Blue Book

Takeaway: Your point of power is now. You can choose how and in which way you proceed and determine the kind of life you will have.

Side Note: Don't be a Henry!

I know I've said it before, but nothing irritates me more than a complainer. I just want to shout, "Well, shut up and do something about it then!" But as that is generally frowned upon, I refrain...

... except when it comes to my husband.

Now on the one hand, I am thankful we can be each other's sounding boards while we are talking things out and looking for solutions; but it's those little complaints that make me go berserk!

And I know I am not supposed to change anyone else. (Well, logically I know this, but sometimes, Alice... to the moon!)

My husband might just be mentioning that the counter is dirty, or the construction down the road has been going on too long, or a co–worker keeps doing something he does not like or whatever. No big deal. It's obviously bothering him. However:

1. He does not seem to be really looking for a solution. I mean, I told him he could wipe the counter and take a different route to work, but he does not seem to want to hear that.

2. It is also NOT my job to make him happy. It is his job to make himself happy. He can either ask me if I have any ideas, ask me wipe off the counter, or do it his damn self! Whew, it does feel good to complain!

With his little complaints, I just HAVE to say something about them or I would burst. I try not to yell at him or make snarky remarks. I just say, "Well, Henry, what are you going to do about that?" (By the way, his real name is Chris.)

So why do I call him Henry?

Do you remember that old folk song, "There's a Hole in the Bucket?" Well, it starts out with Henry singing:

There's a hole in the bucket, dear Liza, dear Liza,
There's a hole in the bucket, dear Liza,
There's a hole.

To which Liza replies:

Then fix it dear Henry, dear Henry, dear Henry,
Then fix it dear Henry, dear Henry,
fix it.

It's the most polite way I can think of to say, "Well then do something about it!" By the way, it goes both ways. He calls me out on this as often as I call him out. (Though he calls me Henrietta.) In turn we are helping each other change our attitudes, from complainers to solution finders.

"I think that the insane desire one has sometimes to bang and
kick grumblers and peevish persons is a Divine instinct."
– Robert Hugh Benson

"No one ever built a monument to a critic."
– George Bernard Shaw

Takeaway: Don't be a Henry! Instead of complaining, do something about it.

Parting thought:

In Man's Search for Meaning Viktor Frankl discusses being in a concentration camp and says, "What alone remains is 'the last of human freedoms' – the ability to 'choose one's attitude in a given set of circumstances.'"

Choose wisely!

Still desiring an Ex?... perhaps, but what are you REALLY desiring?

This may seem like an odd thing to include in a problem solving book, but I have heard enough people sing the same "still desiring an Ex" song, that I feel we must address what is really going on.

I'm going to call the Ex you are still desiring your Ex–Factor. Your Ex–Factors are ex–lovers, ex–significant others, or even ex–friends–you–never–made–a–move–on; a person that part of you wonders if you should be with, because you think you still desire them. Most of us have an Ex–Factor of some kind; the one that got away, or someone from a past relationship that we still think about (especially when Mr. or Mrs. Right Now is annoying the crap out of us). We plague ourselves with "what if's" and torture ourselves with fantasies of what it would be like if only the universe would rearrange itself and we were with our Ex–Factors and we often stop ourselves from creating new loving relationships with new wonderful people because of our hang–ups.

Our society LOVES Ex–Factors and the potential of love re–found. Your little fantasy of the universe rearranging itself is what movies are made of. You know the plot. Mr. Main Character is headed for the altar with Ms. Right Now, but has these nagging thoughts about Ms. Ex–Factor from five years past. So Main Character runs off and makes a fool of himself in several comical ways to try to win Ms. Ex–Factor back and live happily ever after. How many times have we seen that movie?

These movies help fuel your fantasy. It worked for them, why can't it work for me? Hollywood romanticizes our Ex–Factors and tells us that the PURSUIT of love is what it's all about, not love itself. Worse yet, Hollywood has made stalking our Ex–Factors look like the thing you should do to regain your relationship! Do you think I am exaggerating? Read on.

> "A recent study of 180 popular films found no fewer than nine instances per movie of unwanted pursuit. And most of it came off not creepy, but as endearing – and successful... Female pursuers were seen as slightly nutty, but men in that role were seen as charming, and they often got the girl."
> (Psychology Today August 2010)

Here are a couple of examples for you: *There's Something About Mary* (1998), *Twilight* (2008), *My Best Friend's Wedding* (1997), *Maid of Honor* (2008), *Groundhog Day* (1993), *Sleepless in Seattle* (1993), *You've Got Mail* (1998), *27 Dresses* (2007), *As Good as It Gets* (1997), *Serendipity* (2001), *Pretty in Pink* (1986), *Gone with the Wind* (1939) (This one is not a comedy, but there's definitely an Ex–factor going on.) This list could go on and on.

But lets remember, this is Hollywood's version of life. What about REAL life? Well, in real life, if you pursue an Ex–Factor like that you are could end up in jail on stalking charges. OR, you'll end up completely losing all chances with this person. And you'll probably end up scaring away a couple of good potential partners in the process.

What is a person to do? You need to move forward one way or another. So here are some steps to do that:

Step 1 – Put up or shut up!
You know my feelings on this – stop talking and do something. If you REALLY think Mr. or Mrs. Ex–Factor is the one for you, don't stalk them, TELL THEM. Ask them if they feel the same way

you do! If they do, proceed to the "living happily ever after" part.

Scared aren't you? You are telling yourself that it's easier said than done? Well, yes, it is easier said than done, but if you want to live with fulfilled desires, sometimes you have to risk being the fool and take a chance. Or you can just stay in your unfulfilled desire state. The choice is yours.

And, yes, I can speak from experience on this. I have done it. I told Mr. Ex–Factor that I thought he was the one that got away. I had to. Keeping him in my mind was not allowing me to be fully present with anyone else. I knew that one way or another, asking him how he felt would allow me to move forward, either with him or without him.

And, yes, I got my heart stomped on. But I did it, and I didn't have to wonder anymore. Whatever spark I felt, he did not. It... well, sucked, but I am soooo glad I asked. I found out that Mr. Ex–Factor was not the love for me, and I was able to move on.

The point of asking is to move forward in one way or another. If Ex–Factor is not interested in you, it allows you to MOVE ON. No more wondering, and you can proceed to Step 2.

Side Note: If your Ex–Factor is in a relationship, don't even ask. He is not into you! (Read the book He's Just Not That Into You by Greg Behrendt and Liz Tuccillo). If he is in a relationship, proceed directly to Step 2, don't even ask about his feelings – you already know!

Step 2 – Get over it!

That's right, get over your Ex! Let go of the baggage and move on. Okay, give yourself a day to cry, but that's it. Then it's time to accept reality and move on to your yet unimagined, new future.

Clinging to the idea of Mr. Ex–Factor will not get you anywhere. Once you let him go from your heart, you open yourself to the possibility of a new Mr. Right. He might not have the SAME spark as Mr. Ex–Factor, but he could have more and different sparks – enough to sustain a burning fire for a long time. (Did I mention I sometimes call my husband Sparky?)

So how do you get rid of the Ex–Factor in your life? Unscribble THEM! Break them down to the bits and pieces about them that you desire and find other ways to fulfill those experiences! It is not necessarily the Ex–Factor himself that you desire, but the way he or she made you feel.

I read a long time ago that the reason people cheat is often based on how the mistress (or whatever the term for male mistress is) makes the cheater FEEL. "She makes me feel sexy!" "He makes me feel appreciated." It is not necessarily that the cheater has fallen in love, but rather that the mistress makes them feel in a way they desire to feel.

So, the question becomes, "how does Mr. (or Ms.) Ex–factor make you FEEL?"

The Ex–Factor can be one of your biggest clues as to what you desire in life. And a way to turn "getting your heart stomped on" to a jumping point to fulfilling your desires.

Ask yourself, what do you love about her? How did you feel around her? What part of your personality did she bring out in you when you were around her? Get back to the feelings you felt and the experiences you had. Then proceed to finding other ways/people/experiences to fulfill those desires.

Let's look at a few possibilities…

"He made me feel loved"
  – I desire to feel loved
    Get a dog. Start online dating. Visit your grandparents.
    (Stay open to other ideas.)
"She really knew me."
  – I desired to be known and understood.
    Write a book. Share your thoughts with a friend. Start a blog. (Stay open to other ideas.)
"It was the best sex ever."
  – I desire great sex.
    Hire a prostitute… where it's legal. (I'm assuming they'd be good at what they do).
    Find a " buddy." If you are a woman, acquire a good electronic back massager.
    (Stay open to other ideas.)

"She made me feel alive."
  – I desire to feel invigorated.
    Take up sailboat racing. Try hang gliding. (Stay open to other ideas.)
"We could talk for hours."
  – I desire stimulating conversation.
    Join a book club. Go to therapy. Become a therapist. (Stay open to other ideas.)

It MIGHT not necessarily be the Ex–Factor that you desire, rather the feelings and experiences that you had when you were with them. Find out what you enjoyed about your Ex–Factor and explore other ways to fulfill those desires. Who knows, while exploring other ways that make you happy, you might just find a new partner for yourself.

"Every new beginning comes from some other beginning's end."
– Seneca

Takeaway: When you desire someone, it's really the feelings and experiences that you desire. Instead of being stuck on that person, explore other ways to fulfill your desired feelings and experiences.

Side Note: Still desiring a relationship?

If you desire a loving romantic relationship in your life, DO SOMETHING ABOUT IT! But DON'T look for a replica of Ex–Factor, because you won't find it. No two people are alike. And most of the time we should not expect any ONE person to fulfill all of our desires anyway. Explore multiple ways to fulfill your desires. Friendships outside of your romantic relationship can fulfill areas of your life that your significant other might not enjoy. Go to chick flicks with your girlfriends, not your boyfriend. Find a golf buddy so you don't have to listen to your wife complain the whole time when you drag her out to the course. Don't expect all of your desires from a relationship to be fulfilled by one person.

Along the way, your desires may change

Sometimes changes in your life rock your world so much that your desires shift too. Sometimes you fulfill your intentions, then realize you don't desire it anymore. Sometimes your desires simply fade away. Sometimes you just need to acknowledge that the desire, for whatever reason, is no longer there. This is okay. Don't get caught up in seeing something through to the end to the point that you waste your time, energy and resources on something you no longer desire. Perhaps you gained whatever experience your deeper being needed to experience, so your desire has served its purpose.

If your desire is no longer there, think about an exit strategy. My friend Debbie never wanted to retire. She desired and achieved a feeling of fulfillment from doing her work well. She loved working and planned to continue until the day she could not physically do it anymore. Then one day she thought, "I desire to have some adventure in my life; I desire to spend more time with my grandkids; I desire to read more books." She no longer felt fulfilled through her work. So she planned her transition into retirement.

Our desires are present as long as they are present to propel us in that direction. When the direction no longer fulfills our personal development and evolution, the desire will fade. Be okay with that. Accept the change and the new adventure that awaits you. Follow your new desire.

"Make big plans, but change your plans as time changes."
—Marchant

So, just follow your bliss?

I'm not talking about a "giddy happy all the time" kind of bliss. That's nice, but generally not sustainable. True bliss comes from following your desires, or purpose, and living to your potential. Think of bliss more as a sense of well–being than feeling giddy.

As I have said before, follow your desires, but be responsible about it. We are an interdependent species. Whatever people, places or things rely on us should be taken into consideration when you make changes in your life. If you are using the unscribbling process, you should be able to unscribble your desires while still upholding your interdependent responsibilities.

That interdependence may change, but you should be able to find a way to pursue your true desires too. Your desire may need to play out in a different manner than you originally thought, but maybe writing your novel on the weekends instead of quitting your job and writing full time will still do the trick.

But don't ignore that bliss thing either. That blissful energy is pointing you towards something you truly desire. Unscribble it. You will find a way to follow that energy and honor your responsibilities.

*"What man actually needs is not a tensionless state but rather the
striving and struggling for a worthwhile goal, a freely chosen task.
What he needs is not the discharge of tension at any cost but the call
of a potential meaning waiting to be fulfilled by him."*
- Man's Search for Meaning, by Viktor E. Frankl

Takeaway: You can find ways to follow your desires and honor your attachments at the same time. Be responsible as you follow your bliss.

Life is a journey, not a destination

If you cannot be happy until you reach a desire/goal, that's an obsession and you might want to think about seeing a therapist about it. Life is a journey; don't forget to enjoy it along the way.

If you are working toward something you desire, while using your natural gifts and being open to life as it comes your way, the journey will become as enjoyable (if not more enjoyable) than meeting your desire. That's the whole "living life" part. Living life is not about the end result as much as being present and enjoying or loving what is. You may want to make THIS your primary intention.

Most of life is the journey toward our desires, not basking in having achieved them. Think about it. How long do you revel in the glory of a desire fulfilled before a new one crops up? It is natural that as you change and explore life, your desires will also change.

Whatever desires you choose to pursue right now, know that you are not locked in. You can change or tweak them at any time. And you should! As you learn and gather knowledge about your intentions, you will learn more about what you like and don't like about those desires. This allows you to clarify, refine and change your desires as you go – to go with the flow and stay in the moment, instead of deferring your happiness until your desire is fulfilled.

"Success is a journey, not a destination. The doing is often more important than the outcome."
– Arthur Ashe

Takeaway: Remember to enjoy the journey towards your desires as much as when they are fulfilled.

Have patience with yourself

The more you practice unscribbling your desires and problems, the easier it becomes. Like athletes training our bodies, we must train and habituate our minds to SOLVE problems, not get stuck on them. Changing habits takes time.

In the book Outliers, Malcom Gladwell points out that there are no "naturals" at any skill. Everyone must learn or discover how to do something, and then practice the skill or thought pattern before they can look like a natural. He claims that the key to success in any field is a matter of practicing a skill or task for about 10,000 hours. This is true for everyone from the Beatles' music prowess to Tiger Wood's golfing ability.

I doubt that it will take you 10,000 hours to become a good problem solver, but the point is that it takes practice to be a "natural" at anything. With each practice, you get better. Keep practicing till it starts to feel natural; until you get to the point where you don't have to think about solving a problem, you can just naturally move into that mode.

"Think for a moment of a tomato plant... When the first little shoot comes up, you don't stomp on it and say, "That's not a tomato plant." Rather, you look at it and say, "Oh, boy! Here it comes," and you watch it grow with delight. In time, if you continue to water it and give it lots of sunshine and pull away any weeds, you might have a tomato plant with more than a hundred luscious tomatoes. It all began with that one tiny seed."
– You Can Heal Your Life, by Louise L. Hay

Takeaway: Patience is essential. No skill or mind–set comes without practice.

Life gets easier when you can unscribble

Once you see the simple beauty of identifying the desire behind a goal or problem, setting your intention, and opening yourself to the possibilities, you will see that life is not that difficult. You may actually be shocked at how easy it can be. Sometimes you may even realize that you've already fulfilled your desire, just not in the way you thought you were "supposed to" have.

With the right problem solving skills and the knowledge that you deserve for your desires to come to fruition, you will be able to fulfill them – big or small – and unscribble any "problems" or roadblocks that you may face on the journey.

"Focus more on your desire than on your doubt, and the dream will take care of itself. You may be surprised at how easily this happens. Your doubts are not as powerful as your desires, unless you make them so."
– Marcia Wieder

Takeaway: With the right problem solving skills, you can make your dreams and desires come true.

When in doubt

If you are ever not sure what you desire in life, which way to turn, or wonder what we are all here for anyway, try unscribbling the question "How can I feel happy?" Explore where that takes you!

Enjoy the Fish

I once read an article in Worthwhile Magazine by Constance Barkley–Lewis called, "Enjoying the Fish." She writes about some of the struggles we go through in life, and how we choose to deal with them. She likens it to an experience she had while deep-sea fishing, when she got a big fish on her line. While trying to reel it in, she strained her body and got to the point of utter frustration. Then someone came along and simply said to her, "enjoy the fish." Once he said this, she changed her attitude and started to enjoy the process, and the struggle, and she started to enjoy the fish!

Remember, life's struggles can become life's treasures if you change the way you are looking at or dealing with things: if you choose to make the most of a situations; if you choose to enjoy the learning process; if you choose to see the excitement and fun in the struggle; if you choose to enjoy the fish.

It is healthy to strive for things in life, but it is not healthy to deny yourself happiness until your goals are accomplished. Every part of life is to be savored and enjoyed and gained from – even the struggles. Remember to take time and enjoy the fish!

"Not what we have But what we enjoy, constitutes our abundance."
– Epicurus

"Of course life is bizarre, the more bizarre it gets, the more interesting it is. The only way to approach it is to make yourself some popcorn and enjoy the show."
– David Gerrold

Takeaway: You know how to pursue any true desire you have. You know how to handle any problem that comes your way. So enjoy the journey.

Thank you

And to conclude: Thank you! Thank you for taking this journey with me, and for considering my thoughts.

My sincere wish is that you:
- Obtain peace of mind knowing that there are ALWAYS solutions to your problems and ways to attain your true desires.
- Gain confidence knowing that there is more than one solution to whatever situation you are wanting to solve or change.
- Know a step-by-step approach that you can use so you don't have to rely on other people to solve your problems for you.
- Go out into the world with more confidence and with a feeling of worthiness, knowing that you are deserving and capable of making your desires and dreams a reality.
- Find an inner peace and happiness that comes with the confidence of a peaceful mind; and thereby create more inner peace and happiness in the world.

Thank you to all who have helped me write this book. There are too many to thank here, but I do wish to at least thank a few. My husband, Chris Merz, whose encouragement, support and love were instrumental. To my writing group, Dena Mercer and Robin Keene, your advice, edits, talks and overall friendship are invaluable. To Boonabean, my American Bulldog, who always reminds me to love. (She is just so cute you want to hug her and kiss her and call her George every time you see her!) To my friends and testers: Matt Naskrent, Lori Mercer, Karen Kraus, Cher Monfils and Dave Nyman. My editors, Lin Sorenson and Jim Schneider. Mr. Terry Smith for teaching me to love the questions "Why?" and "Why not?" Davie Damkoehler for teaching our Environmental Design class in a discovery learning manner and introducing me to Problem Seeking. To all my family and friends, but especially (and always) to my Mom, Eileen Gutknecht for... everything.

Thank you to the process of writing this book. It was incredibly enjoyable and I learned so much. Thank you for all the struggles that helped me figure out this whole thing, and served as great examples. And of course, thank you to the Universe!!!!

Happy unscribbling, and much love.

Sincerely,
Kristin

"All glory comes from daring to begin."
—Eugene F. Ware

"Twenty years from now you will be more disappointed by the things you didn't do than by the ones you did do. So throw off the bowlines. Sail away from the safe harbor. Catch the trade winds in your sails. Explore. Dream. Discover."
— Mark Twain

Share the love (please):

I like to think of the concept of unscribbling as the little message that could. It's going to be a grassroots effort to get the word out and empower people with a problem solving consciousness. To do that, I can use all the help that I can get.

If you like the book, if you found it helpful or it inspired you in some way, please tell a friend to check it out at http://www.unscribbling.com/share-the-love

Pass on the knowledge of how to solve ANY problem, and have a more easy and enjoyable life today!

Happy Unscribbling!

And, as always, THANK YOU!
This book is self-published. The message about it will primarily be getting out by word of mouth and by my blood sweat and tears (on the side, when I am not working on my design business). So your help in distributing the message and allowing others to learn these helpful problem solving skills is invaluable and so unbelievably appreciated! Thank you again!

Problem Solving for Kids:

I am intending to come out with Unscribbling for Kids, which will be simplified with more child-appropriate examples.

Go to http://www.unscribbling.com and contact us. Let us know you are interested and we will let you know as soon as they are available!

Summary

The Unscribbling Process:

1. BECOME AWARE
You become aware of a problem or area of your life you would like to improve.

2. INTEND
You see what you truly desire and set your intention toward fulfilling that desire.

3. BRAINSTORM
You brainstorm solutions to achieve your desired end state.

4. DECIDE WHICH WAY TO GO
You decide on an option to explore.

5. ACT and EXPLORE
You take action and explore a path or way to get to your desire while staying open to other, possibly better, solutions.

Then, when you solve the problem you...

6. THANK
Giving gratitude for the results, and for everyone who helped you get there.
(P.S. Don't forget to be thanking them all along too.)

Takeaways Recap:

Unscribbling is a problem solving process that empowers you with the ability to tackle any problem that comes your way and to fulfill your dreams.

Once you learn to consciously solve your problems, you will be unstoppable. You will be able to reach all of your true desires.

Step 1 Become Aware

Struggles, or negative feelings, are clues from your internal emotional guidance system encouraging you to make an adjustment.

Wants/goals are just some solutions that can help you meet your true desires.

Goals are rigid benchmarks, desires are helping to guide you to your happiness.

As you work toward your desires in life, stay open to other solutions that might fulfill them.

Instead of resisting the situation that is, embrace it and move toward your true desire from whatever point you are at.

Finding the heart of your problem or desire opens up a world of possibilities to accomplish it.

Work to change ONLY yourself.

A person's desire to change must come from him/herself, not from you.

Intervention in another's life is a drastic step and should not be the sole decision of one individual. If someone is a harm to themselves or others, follow the system of checks and balances to make sure interfering is the correct thing to do.

Be YOURSELF and follow YOUR desires.

Be who you is!

If you desire it, you are worthy of your desire and your desire is worthy of you. Don't let judgment stop you before you even get started.

Behind any perceived desire to harm, there is a deeper desire waiting to be discovered; one with solutions that do not involve violence.

Make sure you are comfortable with your desire before you pursue it.

You are unique. You are beautiful. There is beauty in everyone and everything.

Make your desires unique to you. Use others' examples as your testing ground. Take what you like from each of them. Leave what you don't like.

It's okay to desire to know what your desires are and explore that.

Look for the feeling or experience you are looking for in each desire.

Businesses and employees are helping make other's dreams come true. Clients will choose to work with you (or not) based on the experience you provide them – not merely based on the service or product you provide.

Be sure you can put your desire into the form of a question before you move on.

Pursue the desires that resonate with you and feel right.

Step 2 – Intend

Turn your desire into an intention to empower yourself and excite your mind towards fulfilling your intentions.

Step 3 – Brainstorm (Question)

Turn your intention into a question to put your mind to work searching for solutions.

Be patient with your bee, be patient with yourself, and stay open to new possible solutions that come your way.
Help the "bee" (or yourself) by learning more about whatever you are interested in, and explore other ways to look at the problem or desire. It will help you find more possibilities.

Shifting into thankfulness will help you find even more to be thankful about.

Always stay open to possibilities, even after you have started pursuing a possible solution.

Step 4 – Deciding which way to go?

Whatever solution you decide to explore, know that you are just exploring. You are free to change your mind and explore another solution if the one you choose no longer works.

Your feelings can guide you to the best solution. Follow where they lead.

Engage in no transaction that does not benefit all whom it affects.

Step 5 – Exploring; Transforming the dream(er) to a vision(ary)

Create your "To Do" list by stepping each option back with the questions, "What do I have to do to make this happen?"

By breaking down the path into steps, and taking one step at a time, you will eventually get where you want to be.

Start doing the things on your list.

If you need to take a break from the path for a while, take a break. If you like the path, there is no sense in giving up completely.

Live spherically and pursue as many paths as you can.

If a path no longer feels right, explore another path.

Step 6 – Thank

Remember to thank anyone who has helped you to fulfill your desires.

Part 2

Things to keep in mind on the road while unscribbling

You are worthy of your desires

You must believe you are worthy of having your desires met in order to achieve and hold on to them.

You are worthy. Feeling worthy is a choice. You have the power to feel worthy.

Whatever is in your past is done but you can change your future with your actions in the present. By changing your actions now, you will start to feel worthy.

Start believing that you are worthy. Stop actions, inactions and thinking in ways that make you feel unworthy.

It does not matter what demographic you fit, or what role you played in your past. In this present second, you can choose to live your life differently.

Let your light shine. Inspire others to greatness by example, NOT by holding yourself back.

Using external validation to determine your worth dis–empower you. Empower yourself from the inside out, not the other way around.

Feel worthy and attract opportunities galore!

You don't really desire money

Behind your want for money is a hidden desire. Keep following your wants until you find the experience or feeling you desire.

More money is NOT the only way to fulfill your desires but it is a resource that aids you in fulfilling your desires.

Money is not the source of security, but your ability to solve problems (aka unscribbling) can be. Money is just a resource.

Playing it Safe

Feeling safe and secure does not have to come from sameness. In order to succeed in your desires you will more than likely need to explore something new.

Whatever you imagine your future to look like is not necessarily what the reality will be.

If you are self-sabotaging, you are keeping yourself safe and letting the bogeymen win.

Your life can be and function the way you want it to. Your life does not need to resemble anyone else's life.

The past is past. Learn from it, but consider each situation in its uniqueness and act and risk accordingly.

If you are making excuses and playing the victim, you are keeping yourself in sameness (safe). Accept your situation as it is and then get yourself back on track by unscribbling a new path toward realizing your dreams and desires.

Failure is nothing but a learning experience.

You don't have to take on the "all" of a project. Reverse-bubble things back from your solution and find that first step. Then take it step by step.

If you are procrastinating, you are just keeping yourself safe and avoiding the unknown future – good or bad.

Unknown does not mean unsafe. The unknown could actually be wonderful. But you won't get to explore any of it if you don't take action.

What's the worst that can happen if the worst that can happen happens?

Learn to laugh at yourself. Life is funny, and sometimes we do funny things.

Everyone makes mistakes. Learn from them and move on.

In MOST situations the worst that might happen is not death. If death is a very real possibility, find a different solution to your problem.

When you are afraid to make a move, ask yourself, "What if the worst that can happen happens?" If you can survive that, go for it!

Co–Unscribbling

Involving others in the Unscribbling process will help to create a shared vision and passion.

If you want others to willingly help you achieve your desires, you must ask them to participate.

By acknowledging resistance to solutions you may find ways to clarify your desire or narrow down your solutions.

Let your core desires help you form your group's mission, vision and actions.

When someone presents you with a problem, help them brainstorm and clarify their true desire by asking them if they have considered different solutions instead of telling them what you think they should do.

Welcome Struggles

Struggles, or negative feelings, are clues from your internal emotional guidance system suggesting you make an adjustment.

Make sure the desires you pursue and the ways you are pursuing them are the correct match for you, and that you are not doing things because you feel you are supposed to do them.

Keep exploring, experimenting with and refining your solution until you get exactly what you want. Test, refine, set your new intentions, explore and repeat.

Sometimes it helps to try a different solution to fulfill your desires. If Plan A is not working, try Plan B, or C, or D, or...

Keep your eyes open to new solutions, even when you are focused on your intended solution. A new and better solution might be present itself to you.

Make sure you are on a step in your bubble breakdown that you feel comfortable with. If you aren't, keep breaking the steps down until you get there.

Changing your Attitude

Bad attitudes are not attractive on anyone. Having a good attitude will create more opportunities and give you a better chance of fulfilling your desires.

The fastest way to change your attitude about a problem is to empower yourself by unscribbling it.

Changing the way you look at things can turn apparent negatives into positives, leaving you with a better more productive attitude.

Behind a complainer is someone who desires to be loved, understood and accepted. Changing your attitude and focusing on your desired future will bring you more love, understanding and acceptance than complaining.

Your point of power is now. You can choose how and in which way you proceed and determine the kind of life you will have.

Don't be a Henry! Instead of complaining, do something about it.

Still desiring an Ex?... perhaps, but what are you REALLY desiring?

When you desire someone, it's really the feelings and experiences that you desire. Instead of being stuck on that person, explore other ways to fulfill your desired feelings and experiences.

Along the way, your desires may change

You can find ways to follow your desires and honor your attachments at the same time. Be responsible as you follow your bliss.

Remember to enjoy the journey towards your desires as much as when they are fulfilled.

Patience is essential. No skill or mindset comes without practice.

With the right problem solving skills, you can make your dreams and desires come true.

Enjoy the Fish

You know how to pursue any true desire you have. You know how to handle any problem that comes your way. So enjoy the journey.

Happy Unscribbling!
Much love,
Kristin